PROGRAMMER'S
QUICK
REFERENCE
SERIES

MICROSOFT® C RUN-TIME LIBRARY

□ □ □ □ □

KRIS JAMSA

Microsoft
PRESS
®

PUBLISHED BY
Microsoft Press
A Division of Microsoft Corporation
16011 NE 36th Way, Box 97017, Redmond, Washington 98073-9717

Library of Congress Cataloging-in-Publication Data

Jamsa, Kris A.
Microsoft C run-time library.
1. C (Computer program language)   2. Microsoft C
(Computer program)   I. Title.
QA76.73.C15J358   1989   005.13'3   89-9445
ISBN 1-55615-227-2

Printed and bound in the United States of America.

1 2 3 4 5 6 7 8 9 WAKWAK 3 2 1 0 9

Distributed to the book trade in the United States by Harper & Row.

Distributed to the book trade in Canada by General Publishing
Company, Ltd.

Distributed to the book trade outside the United States and Canada
by Penguin Books Ltd.

Penguin Books Ltd., Harmondsworth, Middlesex, England
Penguin Books Australia Ltd., Ringwood, Victoria, Australia
Penguin Books N.Z. Ltd., 182-190 Wairau Road, Auckland 10,
New Zealand

British Cataloging in Publication Data available

Project Editor: Nancy Siadek
Technical Editor: Dail Magee, Jr.

Introduction

This quick reference guide provides specifics on the Microsoft C Run-Time Library functions. Each entry includes complete syntax, a brief description, details on parameters, and usually a program fragment.

Using the Quick Reference

Each Microsoft C Run-Time Library function is described in the following format:

Function name — **snipe**

Complete syntax (details on next page) — int **snipe**(int *search*);

Required include file(s) — Include file: <shunt.h>

Synopsis of purpose and usage; information about parameters and results —

Description:

snipe searches for the specified numeric index parameter in the current external string.

search is any integer value.

If successful, snipe returns the offset of the numeric index parameter; otherwise, snipe returns the value NOBRD.

Example:
```
#include <stdio.h>
#include <stdlib.h>
#include <shunt.h>

main()
{
    if (snipe(rand()) == NOBRD)
        printf("External string lost\n");
    else
        printf("Numeric index parameter found\n");
}
```

Brief example showing proper usage —

Other functions that are closely related — **Related Functions:** bagstat, strap

Syntax lines use the following conventions:

Convention	*Description*
roman or **bold roman** characters	Enter all roman or bold roman characters as shown, unless they are enclosed in square brackets as explained below.
italics	Italicized names are placeholders for information you must supply, such as a filename or a numeric value.
[*item*]	Items enclosed in square brackets are optional. Exception: A pair of empty brackets ([]) must be entered as shown.
item...	Three dots following an item indicate you can add more items of the same form.

The MS-DOS operating system is referred to as DOS throughout this guide. The Microsoft Operating System/2 multitasking operating environment is referred to as OS/2. The Microsoft C Optimizing Compiler and the Microsoft QuickC Compiler are generally referred to as C.

abort

void **abort**(void);

Include file: <process.h> or <stdlib.h>

Description:

abort ends a program affected by a fatal error or abnormal processing. Upon invocation, abort displays the message

```
Abnormal program termination
```

and returns to DOS an exit code of 3. You can use the DOS IF ERRORLEVEL batch command to test the exit code.

Example:

```
if (count > MAX_ALLOWED)
    abort();
```

Related Functions: exit, _exit, raise, signal, spawnl, spawnle, spawnlp, spawnlpe, spawnv, spawnve, spawnvp, spawnvpe

abs

int **abs**(int *expression*);

Include file: <stdlib.h>

Description:

abs returns the absolute value of an integer expression.

expression is any integer expression whose value is in the range −32,768 through 32,767.

Example:

```
printf("%d %d\n", abs(-3), abs(3));
```

This program fragment produces the following result:

```
-3 3
```

Related Functions: cabs, fabs, labs

access

int **access**(char *pathname*, int *access_mode*);

Include file: <io.h>

Description:

access determines if a file or directory exists on disk and if the program can access the file in the specified mode.

pathname is a character string that contains the DOS path to the desired file or directory.

access_mode specifies the file mode to be checked. Corresponding values and meanings are as follows:

Value	Meaning
0	check only for existence of file
2	check for write permission
4	check for read permission
6	check for read and write permission

access returns the value 0 if the file exists and supports the specified access mode; otherwise, access returns the value −1 and sets the global variable *errno* to one of the following values:

Value	Meaning
EACESS	access denied
ENOENT	file or directory not found

Example:

```
/* see if TEST.DAT exists on disk */

#include <io.h >

main()
{
    if (access("TEST.DAT", 0) == -1)
        {
        printf("TEST.DAT does not exist\n");
        abort();
        }
    /* statements */
}
```

Related Functions: chmod, fstat, open, stat

acos

double **acos**(double *expression*);

Include file: <math.h>

Description:

acos returns the arccosine (0 through π) of an angle specified in radians.

expression is a double-precision expression in the range −1 through 1.

If the expression is outside the range −1 through 1, acos sets the global variable *errno* to the value EDOM (error domain) and sends a DOMAIN error message to stderr.

Example:

```
#include <math.h>

main()
{
    double radians;

    for (radians = -0.5; radians <= 0.5; radians += 0.10)
        printf("%f %f\n", radians, acos(radians));
}
```

Related Functions: asin, atan, atan2, cos, matherr, sin, tan

alloca

void *alloca(size_t *num_bytes*);

Include file: <malloc.h>

Description:

alloca allocates the specified number of bytes within the program's stack space.

num_bytes is an integer expression that specifies the number of bytes to allocate within the stack space.

If successful, alloca returns a pointer to the allocated stack space. If insufficient stack space exists for allocation, alloca returns the value NULL.

Do not use the free function to return space to the stack. Space allocated from the stack is automatically released and returned when the function allocating the space completes execution.

Microsoft C also provides routines that allocate space from the near and far heaps.

Example:

```
#include <malloc.h>
#include <stdio.h>

main()
{
    char *buffer;

    if ((buffer = alloca(1024)) == NULL)
        {
        printf("Insufficient stack space\n");
        abort();
        }
    /* statements */
}
```

Related Functions: calloc, free, malloc, realloc

_arc

short far **_arc**(short *xleft*, short *ytop*,
                 short *xright*, short *ybottom*,
                 short *xstart*, short *ystart*,
                 short *xstop*, short *ystop*);

Include file: <graph.h>

Description:

_arc draws an elliptical arc whose center is the center of the rectangle defined by the coordinates (*xleft*, *ytop*) and (*xright*, *ybottom*). The arc begins at the coordinate where a vector drawn from the center of the arc to the point (*xstart*, *ystart*) intersects the arc. The arc ends at the coordinate where a vector drawn from the center of the arc to the coordinates (*xstop*, *ystop*) intersects the arc.

If successful, _arc returns a nonzero value. If an error occurs, _arc returns the value 0.

Example:

```
#include <graph.h>
#include <stdio.h>

main()
{
    _setvideomode(_MRES16COLOR);
    _arc(10, 10, 50, 50, 0, 0, 100, 100);
    getchar();
    _setvideomode(_DEFAULTMODE);
}
```

Related Functions: _ellipse, _lineto, _pie, _rectangle

asctime

char *__asctime__(struct tm *__datetime__);

Include file: <time.h>

Description:

asctime uses a date and time structure to create a 26-character string that contains the date and time.

datetime is a structure that contains the date and time. It has the following form:

```
struct tm
    {
    int tm_sec;      /* seconds, 0 through 59 */
    int tm_min;      /* minutes, 0 through 59 */
    int tm_hour;     /* hours, 0 through 23 */
    int tm_mday;     /* day of month, 1 through 31 */
    int tm_mon;      /* months since January,
                        0 through 11 */
    int tm_year;     /* years since 1900 */
    int tm_wday;     /* days since Sunday, 0 through 6 */
    int tm_yday;     /* days since January 1,
                        0 through 365 */
    int tm_isdst;    /* 1 if daylight saving */
    };
```

The routines gmtime and localtime each return a structure that contains the date and time.

Example:

```
#include <time.h>

main()
{
    time_t seconds;
    struct tm *current_time;

    time(&seconds);  /* seconds since 01/01/1970 */
    current_time = localtime(&seconds);
    printf("Local time is %s\n", asctime(current_time));
}
```

This program produces the following result:

```
Local time is Tue Dec 20 10:02:49 1989
```

Related Functions: ctime, ftime, gmtime, localtime, time, tzset

asin

double **asin**(double *expression*);

Include file: <math.h>

Description:

asin returns the arcsine ($^-\pi/2$ through $\pi/2$) of an angle specified in radians.

expression is a double-precision expression in the range −1 through 1.

If the expression is outside the range −1 through 1, asin sets the global variable *errno* to the value EDOM (error domain) and sends a DOMAIN error message to stderr.

Example: See acos.

Related Functions: acos, atan, atan2, cos, matherr, sin, tan

assert

void **assert**(int *expression*);

Include file: <assert.h> or <stdio.h>

Description:

assert tests an expression, terminating program execution if the expression is false.

expression is any expression that evaluates to true or false. If the expression is true, program execution continues. If the expression is false, assert displays the following message:

```
Assertion failed: expression, file name, line number
```

and ends program execution.

assert is typically used as a debugging tool.

Example:

```
void str_copy(char *s1, char *s2)
{
    int i;

    for (i = 0; s1[i]; i++)
        s2[i] = s1[i];    /* NULL character is never */
                          /* assigned to the string s2 */
    assert(s2[i] == NULL);
}
```

Related Functions: abort, raise, signal

atan

double **atan**(double *expression*);

Include file: <math.h>

Description:

atan returns the arctangent ($^{-\pi}/2$ through $^{\pi}/2$) of an angle specified in radians.

expression is a double-precision expression.

Example: See acos.

Related Functions: acos, asin, atan2, cos, matherr, sin, tan

atan2

double **atan2**(double *y*, double *x*);

Include file: <math.h>

Description:

atan2 returns the arctangent ($-\pi$ through π) of the expression y/x.

y and x are double-precision expressions.

If both parameter values are 0, atan2 sets the global variable *errno* to the value EDOM (error domain) and sends a DOMAIN error message to stderr.

Example: See acos.

Related Functions: acos, asin, atan, cos, matherr, sin, tan

atexit

int **atexit**(void **function*(void));

Include file: <stdlib.h>

Description:

atexit adds a function to the series of functions that Microsoft C executes after a program completes its execution.

Microsoft C allows you to specify up to 32 functions in a list of functions called an exit list. Microsoft C executes the most recently added function first.

If atexit successfully adds the function to the exit list, it returns the value 0; otherwise, atexit returns a nonzero value.

Example:

```
#include <stdlib.h>

main()
{
    void a(void);
    void b(void);

    atexit(a);
    atexit(b);
    printf("In main\n");
}

void a(void)
{
    printf("In a\n");
}
```

(continued)

```
void b(void)
{
    printf("In b\n");
}
```

This program produces the following result:

```
In main
In b
In a
```

Related Functions: abort, exit, _exit, onexit

atof, atoi, atol

double **atof**(char *str*);

or

int **atoi**(char *str*);

or

long **atol**(char *str*);

Include file: <stdlib.h>

Description:

atof, atoi, and atol convert a character-string representation of a value into the corresponding floating-point value (atof), integer value (atoi), or long value (atol).

These convert the string representation of a value up to the first invalid character or NULL. The routines do not return an error-status value if illegal characters are present in the string.

Example:

```
#include <stdlib.h>

main()
{
    printf("%d %d %d\n", atoi("123"), atoi("12X"),
            atoi("12X3"));
    printf("%f %f\n", atof("123.456"), atof("2.3E4"));
}
```

This program produces the following result:

```
123 12 12
123.456000 23000.000000
```

Related Functions: ecvt, fcvt, gcvt

bdos

int **bdos**(int *dos_function*, unsigned int *dx_register*,
         unsigned int *al_register*);

Include file: <dos.h>

Description:

bdos calls the specified DOS service and returns the value of the AX
register.

dos_function is an integer value that specifies the desired DOS system
service.

dx_register and *al_register* are values bdos assigns to the DX and AL
registers before calling the specified DOS service.

For specific information about DOS system services, see *MS-DOS
Functions: Programmer's Quick Reference* by Ray Duncan, published
by Microsoft Press.

Most current programs use intdos rather than bdos because of the additional flexibility.

Example:

```
#include <dos.h>

main()
{
    /* get DOS version number */
    int version;

    version = bdos(0x30, 0, 0);
    printf("DOS version %d.%d\n", version & 0xff,
           version >> 8);
}
```

Related Functions: int86, int86x, intdos, intdosx

bessel

double j0(double *expression*);

or

double j1(double *expression*);

or

double jn(int *order*, double *expression*);

or

double y0(double *expression*);

or

double y1(double *expression*);

or

double yn(int *order*, double *expression*);

Include file: <math.h>

Description:

The Bessel functions return first-kind and second-kind Bessel functions.

j0, j1, and jn return Bessel functions of the first kind. j0 returns the zero order, j1 returns the first order, and jn returns the order specified by *order*.

y0, y1, and yn return Bessel functions of the second kind. y0 returns the zero order, y1 returns the first order, and yn returns the order specified by *order*.

The expression passed to a Bessel function must be a positive value. If it is not, the function sets the global variable *errno* to the value EDOM (error domain) and sends a DOMAIN error message to stderr.

Example:

```
#include <math.h>

main()
{
    double x = 1.0;
    double y = 2.0;

    printf("j0(1.0) = %f; j0(2.0) = %f\n", j0(x), j0(y));
}
```

This program produces the following result:

```
j0(1.0) = 0.765198; j0(2.0) = 0.223891
```

Related Function: matherr

_bios_disk

unsigned **_bios_disk**(unsigned *service*, structdiskinfo_t **diskinfo*);

Include file: <bios.h>

Description:

_bios_disk provides access to the BIOS disk services through BIOS interrupt 0x13.

service is an unsigned integer that specifies the desired disk service. Valid values and corresponding meanings are as follows:

Value	*Meaning*
_DISK_FORMAT	Formats the specified track
_DISK_RESET	Directs the controller to reset a drive
_DISK_STATUS	Returns the status of the last disk operation. Status values and meanings are as follows:

Value	*Meaning*
0x1	bad request
0x2	address mark not found
0x4	sector not found
0x5	reset operation failed
0x7	drive parameter activity failed
0x9	DMA overrun
0xA	bad sector flag
0x10	data read error
0x11	corrected data read error
0x20	disk controller failed
0x40	seek error
0x80	disk time-out error
0xAA	drive not ready
0xBB	error not defined
0xCC	write fault on drive
0xE0	status error

Value	*Meaning*
_DISK_READ	Reads one or more disk sectors
_DISK_WRITE	Writes one or more disk sectors
_DISK_VERIFY	Examines the specified sectors and performs a CRC test

diskinfo is a structure that contains disk specifics. It has the following form:

```
struct diskinfo_t
    {
    unsigned drive;      /* drive number */
    unsigned head:       /* side number */
    unsigned track;      /* track number */
    unsigned sector;     /* starting sector number */
    unsigned nsectors;   /* number of sectors */
    void far *buffer;    /* I/O buffer */
    };
```

Example:

```
/* copy one disk to another */

#include <bios.h>

main()
{
    int side, track, sector;
    char buffer[512];

    struct diskinfo_t diskinfo;

    diskinfo.nsectors = 1;
    diskinfo.buffer = buffer;

    for (side = 0; side <= 1; side++)
        {
        diskinfo.head = side;
        for (track = 0; track < 40; track++)
            {
            diskinfo.track = track;
            for (sector = 1; sector <= 9; sector++)
                {
                diskinfo.drive = 0;
                diskinfo.sector = sector;
                _bios_disk(_DISK_READ, &diskinfo);
                diskinfo.drive = 1;
                _bios_disk(_DISK_WRITE, &diskinfo);
                }
            }
        }
}
```

Related Functions: _bios_equiplist, _bios_keybrd, _bios_memsize, _bios_printer, _bios_serialcom, _bios_timeofday

_bios_equiplist

unsigned **_bios_equiplist**(void);

Include file: <bios.h>

Description:

_bios_equiplist determines the current hardware configuration through
BIOS interrupt 0x11 and returns values that represent each piece of
equipment.

The bits of the returned unsigned-integer value identify the equipment
in the system. Values and corresponding meanings are as follows:

Bit	*Meaning*
0	1 if a disk drive is installed
1	1 if a math coprocessor is installed
2–3	system board RAM installed (multiples of 16 KB)
4–5	initial video mode
	01 40×25
	10 80×25
	11 80×25 monochrome
6–7	number of floppy-disk drives
	00 = 1 10 = 3
	01 = 2 11 = 4
8	0 if DMA chip is installed
9–11	number of serial ports
12	1 if game adapter is installed
13	1 if serial printer is installed
14–15	number of printers attached

Example:

```
/* check for disks present */

#include <bios.h>

main()
{
    if (1 & _bios_equiplist())
        printf("Disk drives present\n");
}
```

Related Functions: _bios_disk, _bios_keybrd, _bios_memsize,
_bios_printer, _bios_serialcom, _bios_timeofday

_bios_keybrd

unsigned **_bios_keybrd**(unsigned *service*);

Include file: <bios.h>

Description:

_bios_keybrd accesses the BIOS keyboard services through BIOS interrupt 0x16.

service is an unsigned integer that specifies the desired keyboard service. Valid values and corresponding meanings are as follows:

Value	*Meaning*
_KEYBRD_READ _NKEYBRD_READ	Reads a key from the keyboard. If the lower byte of the value is 0, the upper byte contains the scan code of the key pressed.
_KEYBRD_READY _NKEYBRD_READY	Checks to see if a keystroke is waiting to be read, and if so, reads it. If no keystroke is waiting, the return value is 0.
_KEYBRD_SHIFTSTATUS _NKEYBRD_SHIFTSTATUS	Returns the shift-key status in the low-order byte. Meanings of individual bits are as follows:

Bit	*Meaning*
0	Right Shift pressed
1	Left Shift pressed
2	Ctrl pressed
3	Alt pressed
4	Scroll Lock on
5	Num Lock on
6	Caps Lock on
7	Insert mode on

Example:

```
#include <bios.h>

main()
{
    /* wait for a keystroke */
    while (_bios_keybrd(_KEYBOARD_READY) == 0)
        {;}
}
```

Related Functions: _bios_disk, _bios_equiplist, _bios_memsize, _bios_printer,_bios_serialcom, _bios_timeofday

_bios_memsize

unsigned **_bios_memsize**(void);

Include file: <bios.h>

Description:

_bios_memsize returns the amount of system memory in 1 KB blocks. The largest possible value _bios_memsize returns is 640 for 640 KB.

Example:

```
#include <bios.h>

main()
{
    printf("System memory present: %d\n",
        _bios_memsize());
}
```

Related Functions: _bios_disk, _bios_equiplist, _bios_keybrd, _bios_printer, _bios_serialcom, _bios_timeofday

_bios_printer

unsigned **_bios_printer**(unsigned *service*, unsigned *printer_port*,
                                        unsigned *output_data*);

Include file: <bios.h>

Description:

_bios_printer accesses the BIOS printer services through BIOS interrupt 0x17.

service is an unsigned integer that specifies the desired printer service. Values and corresponding meanings are as follows:

Value	Meaning
_PRINTER_INIT	Initializes the specified printer port and returns a status value

(continued)

Value	*Meaning*
_PRINTER_STATUS	Returns the printer status in the low-order byte. Meanings of the individual bits are as follows:

Bit	*Meaning if set*
0	printer timed out
3	output error
4	printer selected
5	out of paper
6	printer acknowledgment
7	printer not busy

Value	*Meaning*
_PRINTER_WRITE	Writes to the printer the character specified by the low-order byte of *output_data* and returns a status value

printer_port specifies the desired printer port. The value 0 indicates LPT1, 1 indicates LPT2, and so on.

The low-order byte of *output_data* contains the characters to be output to the printer.

Example:

```
#include <bios.h>

main()
{
    char *msg = "Printer test";

    while (*msg)
        _bios_printer(_PRINTER_WRITE, 0, *msg++);
}
```

Related Functions: _bios_disk, _bios_equiplist, _bios_keyboard, _bios_memsize, _bios_serialcom, _bios_timeofday

_bios_serialcom

unsigned **_bios_serialcom**(unsigned *service*, unsigned *serial_port*, unsigned *data*);

Include file: <bios.h>

Description:

_bios_serialcom accesses the BIOS serial-communication services through BIOS interrupt 0x14.

service is an unsigned integer that indicates the desired service. Communication services are as follows:

Service	*Meaning*
_COM_INIT	Initializes the communication port using the following constants in the *data* parameter:

Value	*Meaning*
_COM_CHR7	7 data bits
_COM_CHR8	8 data bits
_COM_STOP1	1 stop bit
_COM_STOP2	2 stop bits
_COM_NOPARITY	no parity
_COM_EVENPARITY	even parity
_COM_ODDPARITY	odd parity
_COM_110	baud rate 110
_COM_150	baud rate 150
_COM_300	baud rate 300
_COM_600	baud rate 600
_COM_1200	baud rate 1200
_COM_2400	baud rate 2400
_COM_4800	baud rate 4800
_COM_9600	baud rate 9600

Service	*Meaning*
_COM_RECEIVE	Inputs a character from the communication port
_COM_SEND	Transmits the character specified by the *data* parameter
_COM_STATUS	Returns the current status of the communication port

The high-order byte of the return value contains status flags. Meanings of the individual bits are as follows:

Bit	*Meaning if set*	*Bit*	*Meaning if set*
8	data ready	13	transmission-hold register empty
9	data overrun error		
10	parity error	14	transmission-shift register empty
11	framing error		
12	break detected	15	time-out error

For _COM_INIT and _COM_STATUS operations, the low-order byte of the return value contains additional status flags. Meanings of the individual bits are as follows:

Bit	Meaning if set	Bit	Meaning if set
0	clear-to-send signal toggled	4	clear to send
1	data-set ready signal toggled	5	data-set ready
2	trailing-edge ring indicator	6	ring indicator
3	receive-line signal toggled	7	receive-line signal

serial_port specifies the desired serial port. The value 0 indicates COM1, 1 indicates COM2, and so on.

data indicates either the output data for _COM_SEND operations or the communications parameters for _COM_INIT operations.

Example:

```
#include <bios.h>

main()
{
    /* initialize port COM1 */
    unsigned int status;

    status = _bios_serialcom(_COM_INIT, 0, _COM_CHR8 |
                             _COM_NOPARITY | _COM_4800);
}
```

Related Functions: _bios_disk, _bios_equiplist, _bios_keybrd, _bios_memsize, _bios_printer, _bios_timeofday

---

_bios_timeofday

unsigned **_bios_timeofday**(int *service*, long **clock_val*);

Include file: <bios.h>

Description:

_bios_timeofday accesses the BIOS time-of-day services through BIOS interrupt 0x1A. The BIOS clock monitors time by counting the number of seconds after midnight.

service is an unsigned integer that specifies whether to read or set the current clock time. Time services and corresponding meanings are as follows:

Service	Meaning
_TIME_GETCLOCK	assigns the number of clock ticks to *clock_val*
_TIME_SETCLOCK	sets the clock value to the value in *clock_val*

clock_val is a pointer to a long-integer variable.

Example:

```
#include <bios.h>

main()
{
    long start, current;

    _bios_timeofday(_TIME_GETCLOCK, &start);
    /* delay 5 seconds */
    do
        {
        _bios_timeofday(_TIME_GETCLOCK, &current);
        }
    while ((current - status) <= (5 * 18.2));
}
```

Related Functions: _bios_disk, _bios_equiplist, _bios_keybrd, _bios_memsize, _bios_printer, _bios_serialcom

bsearch

void *__bsearch__(const void *__key_element__, const void *__base_address__,
size_t *num_elements*, size_t *element_width*,
int *compare*(const void *a, const void *b));

Include file: <search.h> or <stdlib.h>

Description:

bsearch is a generic function that performs a binary search on sorted arrays of any type (int, double, and so on) to find a specific value. If bsearch locates the specified value, it returns a pointer to the value; otherwise, bsearch returns the value NULL.

key_element is a pointer to a variable that contains the value for which to search.

base_address is a pointer to the first element in the array.

num_elements specifies the number of elements in the array.

element_width specifies the number of bytes in each element. Use the sizeof operator for this value.

compare is a user-defined function that compares the values referenced by two pointer variables. The function must return a value as follows:

Condition	**Return value**
a > b	a value greater than 0
a == b	the value 0
a < b	a value less than 0

Example:

```
#include <search.h>

main()
{
    int int_array[10];
    float float_array[10];

    int float_comp(float *, float *);
    int int_comp(int *, int *);

    int i, int_key, *int_loc;
    float float_key, *float_loc;

    for (i = 0; i < 10; i++)
        {
        int_array[i] = i;
        float_array[i] = i;
        }

    /* search for the value 3 */
    int_key = 3;
    int_loc = (int *)bsearch(&int_key, int_array,
                             10, sizeof(int), int_comp);
    if (int_loc)
        printf("Value 3 found at %p\n", int_loc);
    else
        printf("Value 3 not found\n");

    /* search for value 7.0 */
    float_key = 7;
    float_loc = (float *)bsearch(&float_key, float_array,
                             10, sizeof(float), float_comp);
    if (float_loc)
        printf("Value 7 found at %p\n", float_loc);
    else
        printf("Value 7 not found\n");
}

int int_comp(int *a, int *b)
{
    return (*a - *b);
}
```

(continued)

```
int float_comp(float *a, float *b)
{
    if (*a > *b)
        return (1);
    else if (*a < *b)
        return (-1);
    else
        return (0);
}
```

Related Functions: lfind, lsearch, qsort

cabs

double **cabs**(struct complex *complex_number*);

Include file: <math.h>

Description:

cabs returns the absolute value of a complex number.

The structure complex is defined as follows:

```
struct complex
    {
    double x;        /* real part */
    double y;        /* imaginary part */
    };
```

cabs calculates the absolute value as follows:

```
result = sqrt(complex.x * complex.x +
              complex.y * complex.y);
```

Example:

```
#include <math.h>

main()
{
    struct complex compnum;

    compnum.x = 5;
    compnum.y = 2;
    printf("Absolute value is %f\n", cabs(compnum));
}
```

Related Functions: abs, fabs, labs

calloc

void ***calloc**(size_t *num_elements*, size_t *element_size*);

Include file: <malloc.h> or <stdlib.h>

Description:

calloc allocates the specified amount of memory from the heap and initializes each element to 0.

If calloc cannot allocate the specified amount of memory, calloc returns the value NULL.

num_elements specifies the number of elements for which to allocate space.

element_size specifies in bytes the size of each element.

Use the free function to return allocated memory to the heap for reuse.

Example:

```
#include <malloc.h>
#include <stdio.h>

main()
{
    /* allocate space for 10 integers */
    int *iptr, i;

    if ((iptr = calloc(10, sizeof(int))) == NULL)
        printf("Insufficient memory available\n");
    else

        {
        for (i = 0; i < 10; i++)
            iptr[i] = i;
        for (i = 0; i < 10; ++i)
            printf("%d\n", iptr[i]);
        free(iptr);
        }
}
```

Related Functions: alloca, free, halloc, hfree, malloc, realloc

ceil

double **ceil**(double *expression*);

Include file: <math.h>

Description:

ceil returns a value of type double that represents the smallest whole number greater than or equal to the specified expression.

expression is any numeric expression.

Example:

```
#include <math.h>

main()
{
    printf("%f becomes %f\n", 0.9, ceil(0.9));
    printf("%f becomes %f\n", 1.1, ceil(1.1));
}
```

This program produces the following result:

```
0.900000 becomes 1.000000
1.100000 becomes 2.000000
```

Related Functions: floor, fmod

cgets

char *cgets(char *str);

Include file: <conio.h>

Description:

cgets reads a string of characters directly from the keyboard.

Before you invoke cgets, you must assign to the first element of the string (*str*[0]) the string size in bytes. Upon completion, cgets places into the second element of the string (*str*[1]) the number of characters actually read. The characters of the string begin at the third element (*str*[2]).

Example:

```
#include <stdio.h>
#include <conio.h>

main()
{
    int i;
    char string[255];
```

(continued)

```
    puts("Enter a string");
    string[0] = 255;
    cgets(string);
    putchar('\n');
    for (i = 0; i < string[1]; ++i)
        putchar(string[i + 2]);
}
```

Related Functions: getch, getche

_chain_intr

void **_chain_intr**(void(interrupt far *_handler_)());

Include file: <dos.h>

Description:

_chain_intr joins one interrupt handler to another.

Many memory-resident programs capture specific interrupts, perform
their own processing, and then pass control on to the original interrupt
handler. The _chain_intr function allows a program to invoke the
original interrupt handler easily.

handler is the far address of the previous interrupt handler. You can
obtain this address using the _dos_getvect function.

Example:

```
#include <dos.h>

void(interrupt far *save_handler)();

main()
{
    void interrupt far my_handler(void);

    save_handler = _dos_getvect(5);
    _dos_setvect(5, my_handler);
    /* program statements */

    /* restore handler */
    _dos_setvect(5, save_handler);
}

void interrupt far my_handler(void)
{
    /* statements */
    _chain_intr(save_handler);
}
```

Related Functions: _disable, _dos_getvect, _dos_keep, _dos_setvect, _enable

chdir

int **chdir**(char *pathname*);

Include file: <direct.h>

Description:

chdir changes the current directory for the specified drive.

pathname is a character string that specifies the desired directory. If you include a disk-drive specifier in *pathname*, chdir selects the directory for the specified drive.

If successful, chdir returns the value 0; otherwise, chdir returns the value −1.

Example:

```
#include <direct.h>

main(int argc, char *argv[])
{
    if (argc > 1)
        if (chdir(argv[1]))
            printf("Error selecting %s\n", argv[1]);
        else
            printf("Directory selected\n");
}
```

Related Functions: mkdir, rmdir

chmod

int **chmod**(char *pathname*, int *permission*);

Include files: <sys\types.h> and <sys\stat.h>

Description:

chmod changes a file's access permission setting.

pathname is a character string that specifies the complete path to the desired file.

permission is an integer value that specifies the desired file access. Valid values are as follows:

Value	*Meaning*
S_IREAD	read-only access
S_IWRITE	write-only access
S_IREAD ¦ S_IWRITE	read and write access

If successful, chmod returns the value 0; otherwise, chmod returns the value −1.

Example:

```
#include <sys\types.h>
#include <sys\stat.h>

main(int argc, char *argv[])
{
    /* set file to read-only */
    if (argc > 1)
        if (chmod(argv[1], S_IREAD))
            printf("Error modifying %s\n", argv[1]);
}
```

Related Functions: access, creat, fopen, fstat, open, stat

chsize

int **chsize**(int *handle*, long *new_size*);

Include file: <io.h>

Description:

chsize changes the size of a file that is associated with the specified file handle.

handle is a file handle associated with a file through the creat or open function.

new_size is a long-integer value that specifies in bytes the desired file size. If the value exceeds the current file size, the file is extended to the specified size and padded with null characters. If the value is less than the current file size, the file is truncated and the data beyond the specified length is lost.

If successful, chsize returns the value 0; otherwise, chsize returns the value −1 and sets the global variable *errno* to the appropriate error-status value.

Example:

```
handle = open("TEST.DAT", O_RDWR);
status = chsize(handle, 1024);
```

Related Functions: creat, open

_clear87

unsigned int _**clear87**(void);

Include file: <float.h> or <math.h>

Description:

_clear87 returns and clears the floating-point status word.

The include file float.h defines the following status values:

Value	Meaning
SW_INVALID	invalid operation
SW_DENORMAL	denormal generated
SW_ZERODIVIDE	division by zero
SW_OVERFLOW	overflow
SW_UNDERFLOW	underflow
SW_INEXACT	result not exact (loss of precision)
SW_UNEMULATED	instruction could not be emulated
SW_SQRTNEG	operation attempted square root of a negative value
SW_STACKOVERFLOW	floating-point stack overflow
SW_STACKUNDERFLOW	floating-point stack underflow

Example:

```
#include <float.h>

main()
{
    printf("Current status word %x\n", _clear87());
}
```

Related Functions: _control87, _status87

clearerr

void **clearerr**(FILE *file_pointer*);

Include file: <stdio.h>

Description:

clearerr resets to zero the error-indicator flag for the specified file.

file_pointer is a file pointer associated with a file through the fdopen, fopen, or freopen function.

The ferror routine detects file errors but does not clear them.

Example:

```
#include <stdio.h>

main()
{
    FILE *fp;
    char buffer[128];
    if ((fp = fopen("TEST.DAT", "r")) == NULL)
        printf("Error opening TEST.DAT\n");
    else

        {
        while (! feof(fp))
            {
            fgets(buffer, sizeof(buffer), fp);
            if (ferror(fp))
                {
                printf("\07Error reading file\n");
                clearerr(fp);
                }
            else
                puts(buffer);
            }
        fclose(fp);
        }
}
```

Related Functions: feof, ferror, rewind

_clearscreen

void far **_clearscreen**(short *screen_area*);

Include file: <graph.h>

Description:

_clearscreen erases either the screen, the graphics viewport, or the text window and fills with the current background color the region of the screen that it clears.

screen_area specifies the region of the screen to clear. Values for screen regions are as follows:

Value	*Meaning*
_GCLEARSCREEN	clears the entire screen
_GVIEWPORT	clears the graphics viewport
_GWINDOW	clears the current text window

Example:

```
#include <graph.h>

main()
{
    _settextwindow(10, 10, 20, 70);
    _clearscreen(_GWINDOW);
    _outtext("Test message");
}
```

Related Functions: _settextwindow, _setviewport

clock

clock_t **clock**(void);

Include file: <time.h>

Description:

clock returns the amount of processor time consumed by the current process.

To determine the number of seconds the program has consumed, divide the value that the clock function returns by the constant CLK_TCK, which is defined in the include file time.h.

Example:

```
#include <time.h>

main()
{
    int i;
```

(continued)

30

```
    for (i = 0; i < 10000; i++)
        {;}
    printf("Processing time: %d\n", clock()/CLK_TCK);
}
```

Related Functions: difftime, time

close

int **close**(int *file_handle*);

Include file: <io.h>

Description:

close closes the file associated with the specified file handle.

file_handle is a file handle associated with a file through the creat or open function.

If successful, close returns the value 0; otherwise, close returns the value −1, indicating an invalid file handle.

Example:

```
#include <io.h>
#include <fcntl.h>

main()
{
    int file_handle;

    if ((file_handle = open("TEST.DAT", O_RDONLY)) == -1)
        printf("Error opening TEST.DAT\n");
    else
        {
        /* statements */
        close(file_handle);
        }
}
```

Related Functions: creat, open

_control87

unsigned int **_control87**(unsigned int *new_controlword*,
                        unsigned int *control_mask*);

Include file: <float.h>

Description:

_control87 returns the current math-coprocessor control word and sets the control word to the value specified.

The floating-point control word allows a program to control precision, rounding, and infinity modes.

new_controlword is the new value for the control word. The include file float.h defines the control-word status values.

control_mask indicates which bits of the control word are to be set. If *control_mask* is 0, _control87 returns only the current control word; otherwise, _control87 updates only those bits of the control word matching the bits of the mask that are currently 1.

Example:

```
#include <float.h>

main()
{
    unsigned int status;

    status = _control87(0, 0);
    printf("Current control word: %x\n", status);
}
```

Related Functions: _clear87, _status87

cos, cosh

double **cos**(double *expression*);

or

double **cosh**(double *expression*);

Include file: <math.h>

Description:

cos and cosh return the cosine of a numeric expression.

expression is a double-precision expression that specifies an angle in radians.

The cosh function returns the hyperbolic cosine.

Example:

```
#include <math.h>

main()
{
    printf("Cosine of pi is %f\n", cos(3.1415926));
}
```

This program produces the following result:

```
Cosine of pi is -1.000000
```

Related Functions: acos, sin, tan

cprintf

int **cprintf**(char *format_string[, output_data]...);

Include file: <conio.h>

Description:

cprintf writes formatted data directly to the console. (The printf function writes data to stdout.)

format_string is a character-string expression containing output-format specifiers. See printf for information about format specifiers.

output_data is an optional list of expressions (separated by commas) that cprintf writes to the screen.

Upon completion, cprintf returns the number of characters it has written to the console.

cprintf does not translate the newline character to the carriage-return–linefeed combination. Instead, you must use \n followed by \r.

Example:

```
#include <conio.h>

main()
{
    int i;

    for (i = 0; i < 10; i++)
        cprintf("%d %d\n\r", i, i * i);
}
```

Related Functions: cscanf, fprintf, printf

cputs

int **cputs**(char *string*);

Include file: <conio.h>

Description:

cputs writes a null-terminated (ASCIIZ) string directly to the console. (The puts function writes data to stdout.)

string is a null-terminated string to be written to the console. If successful, cputs returns the value 0; otherwise, cputs returns a nonzero value.

cputs does not automatically append a carriage-return–linefeed combination to the output string.

Example:

```
#include <conio.h>

main()
{
    cputs("This is all ");
    cputs("displayed on one line\r\n");
}
```

This program produces the following result:

```
This is all displayed on one line
```

Related Functions: putch, puts

creat

int **creat**(char *pathname*, int *permission*);

Include files: <sys\types.h>, <sys\stat.h>, and <io.h>

Description:

creat creates a new file or truncates an existing file, returning a file handle to the file.

pathname is a character string that specifies the complete path of the file to be created.

permission is an integer value that specifies the desired file access. Values and corresponding meanings are as follows:

Value	Meaning
S_IREAD	read-only access
S_IWRITE	write-only access
S_IREAD ¦ S_IWRITE	read and write access

If successful, creat returns the value 0; otherwise, creat returns the value −1 and sets the global variable *errno* to one of the following values:

Value	Meaning
EACCES	pathname specifies a directory or a read-only file
EMFILE	too many open files
ENOENT	path not found

Example:

```
#include <sys\types.h>
#include <sys\stat.h>
#include <io.h>

main()
{
    int handle;

    if ((handle = creat("TEST.DAT",
                        S_IREAD ¦ S_IWRITE)) == -1)
        printf("Error creating file\n");
    else
        close(handle);
}
```

Related Functions: close, open

cscanf

int **cscanf**(char *format_string[, pointer_argument]...);

Include file: <conio.h>

Description:

cscanf reads data directly from the console to the specified variable. (The scanf function reads data from stdin.)

format_string is a character string that specifies the input format. See scanf for format specifiers.

pointer_argument is a list of arguments (separated by commas), each of which is a pointer to a variable.

cscanf returns the number of fields to which it has successfully assigned values. If cscanf attempts to read past the end of file, cscanf returns the value EOF.

Example:

```
#include <conio.h>

main()
{
    int a, b;

    cprintf("Enter two integer values\n\r");
    cscanf("%d %d", &a, &b);
    cprintf("%d and %d\n\r", a, b);
}
```

Related Functions: cprintf, scanf

ctime

char ***ctime**(const time_t **seconds*);

Include file: <time.h>

Description:

ctime converts the number of seconds since midnight on January 1, 1970, Greenwich mean time, to a date/time string.

seconds is a pointer to a variable containing the number of seconds since midnight on January 1, 1970, Greenwich mean time. This value is usually obtained through the time function.

Example:

```
#include <time.h>

main()
{
    time_t seconds;

    time(&seconds);
    printf("%s", ctime(&seconds));
}
```

This program produces the following result:

```
Thu Dec 22 07:45:44 1989
```

Related Functions: asctime, gmtime, localtime, time

dieeetomsbin

int **dieeetomsbin**(double *ieee*, double *msbin*);

Include file: <math.h> or <float.h>

Description:

dieeetomsbin converts a double-precision value stored in IEEE format to Microsoft binary format.

ieee is a pointer to a double-precision value stored in IEEE format.

msbin is a pointer to the variable in which the floating-point value in Microsoft binary format is to be stored.

If successful, dieeetomsbin returns the value 0. If overflow occurs, it returns the value 1.

Related Functions: dmsbintoieee, fieeetomsbin, fmsbintoieee

difftime

double **difftime**(time_t *finish_time*, time_t *start_time*);

Include file: <time.h>

Description:

difftime calculates the difference in seconds between two times. You can obtain values for *finish_time* and *start_time* by using the time function.

Example:

```
#include <time.h>

main()
{
    time_t start_time, finish_time;
    int i, j;

    time(&start_time);
```

(continued)

```
    for (i = 0; i < 10000; ++i)
        for (j = 0; j < 10; ++j)
            {;}
    time(&finish_time);
    printf("Loop required %f seconds",
        difftime(finish_time, start_time));
}
```

Related Function: time

_disable

void _**disable**(void);

Include file: <dos.h>

Description:

_disable disables hardware interrupts until the _enable function is called.

Do not disable interrupts for long periods of time; events that occur while interrupts are disabled will be lost.

Example:

```
#include <dos.h>

main()
{
    void(interrupt far *save_handler)();
    void interrupt far my_handler();

    save_handler = _dos_getvect(5);
    _disable();
    _dos_setvect(5, my_handler);
    _enable();

    /*statements*/

    _disable();
    _dos_setvect(5, save_handler);
    _enable();
}

void interrupt far my_handler(void)
{
    /* statements */
}
```

Related Functions: _chain_intr, _enable

_displaycursor

short far **_displaycursor**(short *on_or_off*);

Include file: <graph.h>

Description:

_display cursor specifies whether the run-time library graphics routines turn the cursor back on when they complete execution. The run-time library graphics routines turn off the graphics cursor upon entry.

on_or_off specifies whether the cursor is to be turned on or left off. The options are as follows:

_GCURSORON	turns cursor on
_GCURSOROFF	turns cursor off

_displaycursor returns the previous value of *on_or_off*.

Example:

```
#include <graph.h>

main()
{
    _setvideomode(_MRES16COLOR);
    _displaycursor(_GCURSOROFF);
    /* statements */
    _setvideomode(_DEFAULTMODE);
}
```

Related Function: _setvideomode

div

struct div_t **div**(int *numerator*, int *denominator*);

Include file: <stdlib.h>

Description:

div divides the numerator by the denominator, returning a structure that contains a quotient and a remainder.

The include file stdlib.h defines the structure div_t as follows:

```
struct div_t
    {
    int quot;
    int rem;
    };
```

Example:

```
#include <stdlib.h>
#include <math.h>

main()
{
    div_t result;

    result = div(15, 4);
    printf("15/4 yields %d with a remainder of %d\n",
            result.quot, result.rem);
}
```

This program produces the following result:

```
15/4 yields 3 with a remainder of 3
```

dmsbintoieee

int **dmsbintoieee**(double *msbin*, double *ieee*);

Include file: <math.h>

Description:

dmsbintoieee converts a double-precision value stored in Microsoft binary format to IEEE format.

msbin is a pointer to a double-precision value stored in Microsoft binary format.

ieee is a pointer to the variable in which the floating-point value in IEEE format is stored.

If successful, dmsbintoieee returns the value 0. If overflow occurs, it returns the value 1.

Related Functions: dieeetomsbin, fieeetomsbin, fmsbintoieee

_dos_allocmem

unsigned **_dos_allocmem**(unsigned *paragraphs*, unsigned **segment*);

Include file: <dos.h>

Description:

_dos_allocmem uses DOS service 0x48 to allocate memory.

paragraphs is an unsigned integer that indicates how many 16-byte paragraphs to allocate.

segment is a pointer to the variable to which the segment descriptor of the beginning paragraph is assigned.

If successful, _dos_allocmem returns the value 0; otherwise, it returns the DOS error code.

Example:

```
#include <dos.h>

main()
{
    unsigned segment, max_avail;

    max_avail = _dos_allocmem(100, &segment);
    if (max_avail)
        printf("No memory allocated\n");
    else
        {
        printf("Memory successfully allocated\n");
        _dos_freemem(segment);
        }
}
```

Related Functions: _dos_freemem, _dos_setblock

_dos_close

unsigned **_dos_close**(int *file_handle*);

Include file: <dos.h>

Description:

_dos_close uses DOS service 0x3E to close the file associated with the specified file handle.

file_handle is a file handle associated with a file through the _dos_creat, _dos_creatnew, or _dos_open function.

If successful, _dos_close returns the value 0. If the handle is invalid, dos_close returns the DOS error code and sets the global variable *errno* to the value EBADF.

Example:

```
#include <dos.h>
#include <fcntl.h>

main()
{
    int file_handle;

    if (_dos_open("TEST.DAT", O_RDONLY, &file_handle))
        printf("Error opening TEST.DAT\n");
    else
        {
        /* statements */
        _dos_close(file_handle);
        }
}
```

Related Functions: _dos_creat, _dos_creatnew, _dos_open

_dos_creat

unsigned **_dos_creat**(char *pathname*, unsigned *attribute*,
                    int **file_handle*);

Include file: <dos.h>

Description:

_dos_creat uses DOS service 0x3C to create a file. If the file already exists, _dos_creat overwrites it.

pathname is a character string that contains the complete path to the desired file.

attribute is an unsigned integer that specifies the desired file attributes. Valid values and corresponding meanings are as follows:

Value	Meaning
_A_NORMAL	normal file access
_A_RDONLY	read-only access
_A_HIDDEN	hidden file
_A_SYSTEM	system file
_A_VOLID	volume label
_A_SUBDIR	subdirectory
_A_ARCH	archive required

file_handle is a pointer to the variable to which the file handle is assigned.

If successful, _dos_creat returns the value 0. If an error occurs, _dos_creat returns the DOS error code and sets the global variable *errno* to one of the following values:

Value	*Meaning*
EACESS	access denied. File might already exist and be read-only
EEXIST	file or subdirectory already exists
EMFILE	too many open files
ENOENT	path or file not found

Example:

```
#include <dos.h>

main()
{
    int file_handle;

    if (_dos_creat("TEST.DAT", _A_NORMAL, &file_handle))
        printf("Error creating TEST.DAT\n");
    else
        {
        /* statements */
        _dos_close(file_handle);
        }
}
```

Related Functions: _dos_close, _dos_creatnew, _dos_open

_dos_creatnew

unsigned **_dos_creatnew**(char *pathname*, unsigned *attribute*,
                             int *file_handle*);

Include file: <dos.h>

Description:

_dos_creatnew uses DOS service 0x5B to create a file. If a file with the specified name already exists, _dos_creatnew fails. See _dos_creat for information on parameters and return values.

Example: See _dos_creat.

Related Functions: _dos_close, _dos_creat, _dos_open

dosexterr

int **dosexterr**(struct DOSERROR ∗*error_info*);

Include file: <dos.h>

Description:

dosexterr uses DOS service 0x59 to obtain extended error information about a DOS error.

error_info is a pointer to a structure containing extended error information, defined in the include file dos.h as follows:

```
struct DOSERROR
    {
    int exterror;    /* extended error code */
    char class;      /* error class */
    char action;     /* recommended action */
    char locus;      /* probable cause */
    };
```

For specifics on error handling in Microsoft C, refer to my book *Microsoft C: Secrets, Shortcuts, and Solutions,* published by Microsoft Press.

Example:

```
void error_handler(void)
{
    struct DOSERROR error_info;

    dosexterr(&error_info);
    printf("Error %d  Class %d  Action %d  Locus %d\n",
           error_info.exterror, error_info.class,
           error_info.action, error_info.locus);
}
```

_dos_findfirst

unsigned **_dos_findfirst**(char ∗*pathname*, unsigned *attribute*,
                        struct find_t ∗*fileinfo*);

Include file: <dos.h>

Description:

_dos_findfirst uses DOS service 0x4E to locate the first instance of a file whose name and attributes match the specified pathname and attributes.

pathname is a character string that contains the desired file specification. If *pathname* contains wildcard characters, _dos_findfirst returns the first matching file.

attribute is an unsigned integer that specifies the file attributes of the desired file. Valid values and corresponding meanings are as follows:

Value	*Meaning*
_A_NORMAL	normal file
_A_RDONLY	read-only file
_A_HIDDEN	hidden file
_A_SYSTEM	system file
_A_VOLID	volume label
_A_SUBDIR	subdirectory
_A_ARCH	archive required

fileinfo is a pointer to a structure of type find_t, defined in the include file dos.h as follows:

```
struct find_t
    {
    char reserved[21];
    char attrib;
    unsigned wr_time;      /* time stamp */
    unsigned wr_date;      /* date stamp */
    long size;             /* size in bytes */
    char name[13]          /* name.ext */
    };
```

_dos_findfirst and _dos_findnext work as a team to perform directory-wide file operations. _dos_findfirst finds the first matching file, and _dos_findnext locates successive files.

If successful, _dos_findfirst returns the value 0. If an error occurs (such as no matching file), _dos_findfirst returns the DOS error code and sets the global variable *errno* to the value ENOENT.

Example:

```
#include <dos.h>

main()
{
    /* display files in the current directory */
    struct find_t fileinfo;
    int status;

    status = _dos_findfirst("*.*", _A_NORMAL, &fileinfo);
    while (status == 0)
        {
        puts(fileinfo.name);
        status = _dos_findnext(&fileinfo);
        }
}
```

Related Function: _dos_findnext

_dos_findnext

unsigned **_dos_findnext**(struct find_t *fileinfo*);

Include file: <dos.h>

Description:

_dos_findnext uses DOS service 0x4F to locate successive files that match the specified pathname and attributes in a previous call to the _dos_findfirst function.

fileinfo is a pointer to a structure of type find_t, defined in the include file dos.h. See _dos_findfirst for further information.

If successful, _dos_findnext returns the value 0; otherwise, the _dos_findnext function returns the DOS error code and sets the global variable *errno* to the value ENOENT.

Example: See _dos_findfirst.

Related Function: _dos_findfirst

_dos_freemem

unsigned **_dos_freemem**(unsigned *segment*);

Include file: <dos.h>

Description:

_dos_freemem uses DOS service 0x49 to release memory allocated by the _dos_allocmem function.

segment is an unsigned integer that contains\the segment descriptor for a block of memory previously allocated by the _dos_allocmem or _dos_setblock functions.

If successful, _dos_freemem returns the value 0; otherwise, the _dos_freemem function returns the DOS error code and sets the global variable *errno* to the value ENOMEM.

Example: See _dos_allocmem.

Related Functions: _dos_allocmem, _dos_setblock

_dos_getdate

void **_dos_getdate**(struct dosdate_t *date*);

Include file: <dos.h>

Description:

_dos_getdate uses DOS service 0x2A to obtain the current system date.

date is a pointer to a structure that is defined in the include file dos.h as follows:

```
struct dosdate_t
    {
    unsigned char day;
    unsigned char month;
    unsigned int year;
    unsigned char dayofweek;
    };
```

Example:

```
#include <dos.h>

main()
{
    struct dosdate_t date;

    _dos_getdate(&date);
    printf("Current date: %d-%d-%d\n", date.month,
        date.day, date.year);
}
```

This program produces the following result:

```
Current date: 12/25/1989
```

Related Functions: _dos_gettime, _dos_setdate, _dos_settime

_dos_getdiskfree

unsigned **_dos_getdiskfree**(unsigned *disk_drive*,
struct diskfree_t **diskinfo*);

Include file: <dos.h>

Description:

_dos_getdiskfree uses DOS service 0x36 to obtain disk-storage information for the specified disk drive.

disk_drive is an unsigned integer that represents the desired disk drive. The value 0 indicates the current drive, 1 indicates drive A, 2 indicates drive B, and so on.

diskinfo is a pointer to a structure of type diskfree_t, defined in the include file dos.h as follows:

```
struct diskfree_t
    {
    unsigned total_clusters;
    unsigned avail_clusters;
    unsigned sectors_per_cluster;
    unsigned bytes_per_sector;
    };
```

If successful, _dos_getdiskfree returns the value 0; if the disk drive specified is invalid, _dos_getdiskfree returns the DOS error code and sets the global variable *errno* to the value EINVAL.

Example:

```
#include <dos.h>

main()
{
    struct diskfree_t diskinfo;
    long space;

    _dos_getdiskfree(0, &diskinfo);
    space = (long)diskinfo.total_clusters *
            (long)diskinfo.sectors_per_cluster *
            (long)diskinfo.bytes_per_sector;
    printf("Total disk space is %ld\n", space);
}
```

Related Functions: _dos_getdrive, _dos_setdrive

_dos_getdrive

void _**dos_getdrive**(unsigned int *drive*);

Include file: <dos.h>

Description:

_dos_getdrive uses DOS service 0x19 to obtain the current disk-drive
number (0 = A, 1 = B, 2 = C, and so on).

Example:

```
#include <dos.h>

main()
{
    unsigned int drive;

    _dos_getdrive(&drive);
    printf("Current drive is %d\n", drive);
}
```

Related Function: _dos_setdrive

_dos_getfileattr

unsigned _**dos_getfileattr**(char *pathname*, unsigned *attribute*);

Include file: <dos.h>

Description:

_dos_getfileattr uses DOS service 0x43 to obtain the file attributes for
the specified file.

pathname is a character string that contains the complete path to the
desired file.

attribute is a pointer to a variable to which the file attributes are assigned. The low-order byte of the attribute word can contain the following values:

Value	Meaning
_A_NORMAL	normal file
_A_RDONLY	read-only file
_A_HIDDEN	hidden file
_A_SYSTEM	system file
_A_VOLID	volume label
_A_SUBDIR	subdirectory
_A_ARCH	archive required

If successful, _dos_getfileattr returns the value 0; otherwise, the _dos_getfileattr function returns the DOS error code and sets the global variable *errno* to the value ENOENT.

Example:

```
#include <dos.h>

main(int argc, char *argv[])
{
    int attribute;

    if (_dos_getfileattr(argv[1], &attribute))
        printf("Error accessing %s\n", argv[1]);
    else
        {
        if (attribute == _A_NORMAL)
            printf("Normal file\n");
        if (attribute & _A_RDONLY)
            printf("Read-only\n");
        if (attribute & _A_HIDDEN)
            printf("Hidden\n");
        if (attribute & _A_VOLID)
            printf("Volume label\n");
        if (attribute & _A_SUBDIR)
            printf("Subdirectory\n");
        if (attribute & _A_ARCH)
            printf("Archive\n");
        }
}
```

Related Function: _dos_setfileattr

_dos_getftime

unsigned **_dos_getftime**(int *file_handle*, unsigned int *date*, unsigned int *time*);

Include file: <dos.h>

Description:

_dos_getftime uses DOS service 0x57 to obtain a file's date and time stamp.

file_handle is a file handle associated with a file through the _dos_open function.

date is a pointer to an unsigned integer whose bits represent the date, as follows:

Bits	*Date field*
0–4	day (1 through 31)
5–8	month (1 through 12)
9–15	year (1980 through 2099)

time is a pointer to an unsigned integer whose bits represent the current time, as follows:

Bits	*Time field*
0–4	seconds divided by 2 (0 through 29)
5–10	minutes (0 through 59)
11–15	hours (0 through 23)

If successful, _dos_getftime returns the value 0; if the file handle is invalid, _dos_getftime returns the DOS error code and sets the global variable *errno* to the value EBADF.

Example:

```
#include <dos.h>
#include <fcntl.h>

main()
{
    int handle, year, day, month, hour, minute, second;
    unsigned date, time;

    if (_dos_open("TEST.DAT", O_RDWR, &handle) != 0)
        printf("Error opening TEST.DAT\n");
    else
        {
        _dos_getftime(handle, &date, &time);
        year = (date >> 9) + 1980;
        month = (date & 0x1E0) >> 5;
        day = date & 0x1F;
        hour = time >> 11;
        minute = (time & 0x7E0) >> 5;
        second = (time & 0x1F) * 2;
        printf("TEST.DAT %d-%d-%d %d:%d:%d\n",
                month, day, year, hour, minute, second);
        }
}
```

Related Function: _dos_setftime

_dos_gettime

void **_dos_gettime**(struct dostime_t *time);

Include file: <dos.h>

Description:

_dos_gettime uses DOS service 0x2C to obtain the current system time.

time is a pointer to a structure of type dostime_t, defined in the include file dos.h as follows:

```
struct dostime_t
    {
    unsigned char hour;
    unsigned char minute;
    unsigned char second;
    unsigned char hsecond;
    };
```

Example:

```
#include <dos.h>

main()
{
    struct dostime_t time;

    _dos_gettime(&time);
    printf("Current time: %d:%d:%d.%d\n",
            time.hour, time.minute, time.second,
            time.hsecond);
}
```

Related Functions: _dos_getdate, _dos_setdate, _dos_settime

_dos_getvect

void(interrupt far *_dos_getvect(unsigned *interrupt_num*))();

Include file: <dos.h>

Description:

_dos_getvect uses DOS service 0x35 to obtain the interrupt vector for the specified interrupt.

interrupt_num is an unsigned integer that specifies the desired interrupt.

Example: See _chain_intr.

Related Functions: _chain_intr, _dos_setvect

_dos_keep

void **_dos_keep**(unsigned *return_code*, unsigned *num_paragraphs*)

Include file: <dos.h>

Description:

_dos_keep uses DOS service 0x31 to install a memory-resident program.

return_code is the status code to be returned to the parent of the calling process.

num_paragraphs is an unsigned integer that indicates how many 16-byte paragraphs to allocate for the program's use.

Related Functions: _chain_intr, _dos_getvect, _dos_setvect

_dos_open

unsigned **_dos_open**(char *pathname*, unsigned *access_mode*,
                       int *file_handle*);

Include file: <dos.h>

Description:

_dos_open uses DOS service 0x3D to open an existing file and returns a handle to the file.

pathname is a character string that contains the complete path to the desired file.

access_mode is an unsigned integer that specifies how the program will access the file. Valid values and corresponding meanings are as follows:

Value	Meaning
O_RDONLY	read-only access
O_WRONLY	write-only access
O_RDWR	read and write access
O_NOINHERIT	child process cannot inherit the file handle
SH_COMPAT	compatibility sharing
SH_DENYRW	deny read/write sharing
SH_DENYWR	deny write sharing
SH_DENYRD	deny read sharing
SH_DENYNO	allow read/write sharing

file_handle is a pointer to an integer variable to which the file handle is assigned.

If successful, _dos_open returns the value 0; otherwise, _dos_open returns the DOS error code and sets the global variable *errno* to one of the following values:

Value	Meaning
EACESS	access denied
EINVAL	access mode is invalid
EMFILE	too many open files
ENOENT	path or file not found

Example:

```
#include <dos.h>
#include <fcntl.h>

main()
{
    int file_handle;

    if (_dos_open("TEST.DAT", O_RDONLY, &file_handle))
        printf("Error opening TEST.DAT\n");
    else
        {
        /* statements */
        _dos_close(file_handle);
        }
}
```

Related Functions: _dos_close, _dos_creat, _dos_creatnew

_dos_read

int **dos_read**(int *file_handle*, void far *buffer*,
                 unsigned *num_bytes*, unsigned *bytes_read*);

Include file: <dos.h>

Description:

_dos_read uses DOS service 0x3F to read the specified number of
bytes from a file into an input buffer.

file_handle is a file handle associated with a file through the
_dos_open function.

buffer is a pointer to the starting address of an input buffer into which
_dos_read reads the data.

num_bytes is an unsigned integer that indicates the number of bytes to
be read.

bytes_read is a pointer to a variable to which _dos_read assigns the
actual number of bytes read from the file.

If successful, _dos_read returns the value 0; otherwise, it returns the
DOS error code and sets the global variable *errno* to one of the following values:

Value	*Meaning*
EBADF	invalid file handle
EACCES	file access denied

Example:

```
#include <dos.h>
#include <fcntl.h>

main(int argc, char *argv[])
{
    int input, output, bytes_read, bytes_written;
    char buffer[512];

    if (argc < 3)
        printf("Must specify source and target files\n");
    else
        {
        if (_dos_open(argv[1], O_RDONLY, &input) != 0)
            printf("Error opening %s\n", argv[1]);
```

(continued)

55

```
else if (_dos_open(argv[2],
                   O_WRONLY, &output) != 0)
    printf("Error opening %s\n", argv[2]);
else
    {
    do
        {
        _dos_read(input, buffer, sizeof(buffer),
                &bytes_read);
        _dos_write(output, buffer, bytes_read,
                &bytes_written);
        }
    while (bytes_read != 0);
    _dos_close(input);
    _dos_close(output);
    }
    }
}
```

Related Functions: dos_close, dos_open, dos_write

_dos_setblock

unsigned **_dos_setblock**(unsigned int *new_size*,
                    unsigned int *segment*,
                    unsigned int *max_mem*);

Include file: <dos.h>

Description:

_dos_setblock uses DOS service 0x4A to change the size of a block of
memory previously allocated through the _dos_allocmem function.

new_size is an unsigned integer that indicates in 16-byte paragraphs
the desired size of the block of memory.

segment is the segment address of the start of the memory block.

max_mem is a pointer to an unsigned integer variable to which
_dos_setblock assigns the size of the largest available block of
memory.

If successful, _dos_setblock returns the value 0; otherwise, the
_dos_setblock function returns the DOS error code and sets the global
variable *errno* to the value ENOMEM.

Example:

```
#include <dos.h>
```

(continued)

```
main()
{
    unsigned int segment, max_mem;

    if (_dos_allocmem(10, &segment))
        printf("Error allocating memory\n");
    else
        {
        if (_dos_setblock(20, segment, &max_mem))
            printf("Max available memory: %u\n",
                    max_mem);
        else
            printf("Allocation set to 20\n");
        _dos_freemem(segment);
        }
}
```

Related Functions: _dos_allocmem, _dos_freemem

_dos_setdate

unsigned **_dos_setdate**(struct dosdate_t *date);

Include file: <dos.h>

Description:

_dos_setdate uses DOS service 0x2B to set the system date.

date is a pointer to a structure of type dostime_t, defined in the include file dos.h as follows:

```
struct dosdate_t
    {
    unsigned char day;
    unsigned char month;
    unsigned int year;
    unsigned char dayofweek;
    };
```

If successful, _dos_setdate returns the value 0; otherwise, _dos_setdate returns the DOS error code and sets the global variable *errno* to the value EINVAL.

Example:

```
#include <dos.h>
```

(continued)

```
main()
{
    struct dosdate_t date;

    /* set date to 12/25/89 */
    date.month = 12;
    date.day = 25;
    date.year = 1989;
    if (_dos_setdate(&date))
        printf("Error setting date\n");
    else
        printf("Date set to 12/25/89\n");
}
```

Related Functions: _dos_getdate, _dos_gettime, _dos_settime

_dos_setdrive

void **_dos_setdrive**(unsigned int *disk_drive*,
                       unsigned int **drives_avail*);

Include file: <dos.h>

Description:

_dos_setdrive uses DOS service 0x0E to set the current disk drive.

disk_drive is an unsigned integer value that indicates the desired disk drive. The value 1 indicates drive A, 2 indicates drive B, and so on.

drives_avail is a pointer to an unsigned integer variable to which _dos_setdrive assigns the number of available drives.

Example:

```
#include <dos.h>

main()
{
    unsigned int drives_avail;

    /* select drive A */
    _dos_setdrive(1, &drives_avail);
    printf("Number of available drives: %d\n",
            drives_avail);
}
```

Related Function: _dos_getdrive

_dos_setfileattr

unsigned **_dos_setfileattr**(char *pathname*, unsigned int *attributes*);

Include file: <dos.h>

Description:

_dos_setfileattr uses DOS service 0x43 to set a file's attributes.

pathname is a character string that contains the complete path to the desired file.

attributes is an unsigned integer value that indicates the desired file attributes. See _dos_getfileattr for valid values.

If successful, _dos_setfileattr returns the value 0; otherwise, the _dos_setfileattr function returns the DOS error code and sets the global variable *errno* to one of the following values:

Value	Meaning
ENOENT	file or path not found
EACCES	access denied

Example:

```
#include <dos.h>

main(int argc, char *argv[])
{
    if (argc > 1)
        if (_dos_setfileattr(argv[1], _A_RDONLY))
            printf("Error changing %s\n", argv[1]);
        else
            printf("%s set to read-only\n", argv[1]);
}
```

Related Function: _dos_getfileattr

_dos_setftime

unsigned **_dos_setftime**(int *file_handle*, unsigned int *date*,
                          unsigned int *time*);

Include file: <dos.h>

Description:

_dos_settime uses DOS service 0x57 to set a file's date and time stamp.

file_handle is a file handle associated with a file through the _dos_open function.

date is an unsigned integer whose bits indicate the desired date, as follows:

Bits	*Date field*
0–4	day (1 through 31)
5–8	month (1 through 12)
9–15	year (1980 through 2099)

time is an unsigned integer whose bits specify the desired time, as follows:

Bits	*Time field*
0–4	seconds divided by 2 (0 through 29)
5–10	minutes (0 through 59)
11–15	hours (0 through 23)

If successful, _dos_settime returns the value 0; otherwise, the _dos_settime function returns the DOS error code and sets the global variable *errno* to the value EBADF.

Example:

```
#include <dos.h>
#include <fcntl.h>

main()
{
    int handle, year = 1989, month = 12, day = 25;
    int hour = 12, minute = 30, second = 40;
    unsigned date, time;

    if (_dos_open("TEST.DAT", O_RDWR, &handle) != 0)
        printf("Error opening TEST.DAT\n");
    else
        {
        date = (year - 1980) << 9;
        date += month << 5;
        date += day;
        time = hour << 11;
        time += minute << 5;
        time += second / 2;
        _dos_settime(handle, date, time);
        }
}
```

Related Function: _dos_getftime

_dos_settime

unsigned **_dos_settime**(struct dostime_t *time*);

Include file: <dos.h>

Description:

_dos_settime uses DOS service 0x2D to set the current system time.

time is a pointer to a structure of type dostime_t, defined in the include file dos.h as follows:

```
struct dostime_t
    {
    unsigned char hour;
    unsigned char minute;
    unsigned char second;
    unsigned char hsecond;
    };
```

If successful, _dos_settime returns the value 0; otherwise, the _dos_settime function returns the DOS error code and sets the global variable *errno* to the value EINVAL.

Example:

```
#include <dos.h>

main()
{
    struct dostime_t time;

    /* set time to 12:30:00 */
    time.hour = 12;
    time.minute = 30;
    time.second = 0;
    if (_dos_settime(&time))
        printf("Error setting time\n");
    else
        printf("Time set to 12:30\n");
}
```

Related Functions: _dos_getdate, _dos_gettime, _dos_setdate

_dos_setvect

void **_dos_setvect**(unsigned int *interrupt_num*,
                void (interrupt far *handler*)());

Include file: <dos.h>

Description:

_dos_setvect uses DOS service 0x25 to assign a new interrupt vector to the specified interrupt.

interrupt_num is an unsigned integer value that indicates the desired interrupt.

handler is a pointer to a function that serves as the new interrupt handler.

Example: See _chain_intr.

Related Functions: _chain_intr, _dos_getvect

_dos_write

unsigned **_dos_write**(int *file_handle*, void far **buffer*,
              unsigned int *num_bytes*,
              unsigned int **bytes_written*);

Include file: <dos.h>

Description:

_dos_write uses DOS service 0x40 to write data from an output buffer to the specified file.

file_handle is a file handle associated with a file through the _dos_creat, _dos_creatnew, or _dos_open function.

num_bytes is an unsigned integer value that indicates the number of bytes to write.

bytes_written is a pointer to an unsigned integer variable to which _dos_write assigns the number of bytes actually written.

If successful, _dos_write returns the value 0; otherwise, _dos_write returns the DOS error code and sets the global variable *errno* to one of the following values:

Value	Meaning
EBADF	invalid file handle
EACCES	access denied

Example: See _dos_read.

Related Functions: _dos_close, _dos_open, _dos_read

dup

int **dup**(int *file_handle*);

Include file: <io.h>

Description:

dup assigns a second file handle to an open file.

file_handle is a file handle associated with an open file.

If successful, dup returns a new file handle. If an error occurs, dup returns the value −1 and sets the global variable *errno* to one of the following values:

Value	Meaning
EBADF	invalid file handle
EMFILE	too many open files

Example:

```
#include <io.h>

main()
{
    int save_handle;

    save_handle = dup(1);   /* dup stdout */
    /* statements */
}
```

Related Functions: close, dup2, open

dup2

int **dup2**(int *source_handle*, int *target_handle*);

Include file: <io.h>

Description:

dup2 associates a file handle with a file pointed to by another file handle.

source_handle is an existing file handle.

target_handle is a file handle that will point to the same file as *source_handle*. If *target_handle* already points to a file, dup2 closes the file.

If successful, dup2 returns the value 0. If an error occurs, dup2 returns the value −1 and sets the global variable *errno* to one of the following values:

Value	*Meaning*
EBADF	invalid file handle
EMFILE	too many open files

Example:

```
/* write all output to stderr instead of */
/* stdout to prevent DOS from redirecting it */

#include <io.h>
#include <stdio.h>

main()
{
    int old_handle, letter;

    if ((old_handle = dup(fileno(stdout))) == -1)
        printf("Error duplicating stdout\n");
    else
        {
        if (dup2(fileno(stderr), fileno(stdout)) == -1)
            printf("Error duplicating stderr\n");
        else
            {
            for (letter = 'A'; letter <= 'Z'; letter++)
                putchar(letter);
            if (dup2(old_handle, fileno(stdout)) == -1)
                printf("Error reassigning stdout\n");
            }
        }
}
```

Related Functions: close, dup, open

ecvt

char *__ecvt__(double *expression*, int *count*, int *decimal_pos*,
        int *sign*);

Include file: <stdlib.h>

Description:

ecvt converts a floating-point expression to a character string, assigning only the digits to the string. ecvt returns the position of the decimal point but does not place the decimal point into the string.

expression is a double-precision expression to be converted into a character string.

count indicates the number of digits to be placed in the string.

decimal_pos is a pointer to an integer variable to which ecvt assigns the position of the decimal point.

sign is a pointer to an integer variable to which ecvt assigns the sign. If *sign* is 0, *expression* was positive; otherwise, *expression* was negative.

Example:

```
#include <stdlib.h>
#include <stdio.h>

main()
{
    double x = 1.23456789;
    char *string;
    int decimal_pos, sign;

    string = ecvt(x, 9, &decimal_pos, &sign);
    printf("%s  Sign %d  Decimal position %d\n",
            string, sign, decimal_pos);
}
```

This program produces the following result:

```
123456789  Sign 0  Decimal position 1
```

Related Functions: atof, atoi, atol, fcvt, gcvt

_ellipse

short **far** _ellipse(short *fill_flag*, short *x_left*, short *y_top*,
                short *x_right*, short *y_bottom*);

Include file: <graph.h>

Description:

_ellipse draws an ellipse in the region bounded by a rectangle that is defined by the coordinates (*x_left*, *y_top*) and (*x_right*, *y_bottom*).

fill_flag is a short value that indicates whether the ellipse is filled. Values and meanings are as follows:

Value	*Meaning*
_GBORDER	do not fill ellipse
_GFILLINTERIOR	fill ellipse

If successful, _ellipse returns a nonzero value. If an error occurs, _ellipse returns the value 0.

Example:

```
#include <graph.h>
#include <stdio.h>

main()
{
    _setvideomode(_MRES16COLOR);
    _ellipse(_GFILLINTERIOR, 10, 10, 50, 50);
    getchar();
    _setvideomode(_DEFAULTMODE);
}
```

Related Functions: _arc, _pie, _setvideomode

_enable

void **_enable**(void);

Include file: <dos.h>

Description:

_enable enables the hardware interrupts that were previously disabled by the _disable function.

Example: See _disable.

Related Functions: _chain_intr, _disable

eof

int **eof**(int *file_handle*);

Include file: <io.h>

Description:

eof tests whether the file associated with the specified file handle has reached end-of-file (EOF).

file_handle is a file handle associated with a file through the creat or open function.

eof returns the value 1 if the file is currently at end-of-file or −1 if
file_handle is invalid; otherwise, eof returns the value 0.

Example:

```
#include <io.h>
#include <fcntl.h>

main(int argc, char *argv[])
{
    int file_handle;
    int bytes_read;
    char buffer[128];

    if ((file_handle = open(argv[1], O_RDONLY)) == -1)
        printf("Error opening %s\n", argv[1]);
    else
        {
        while (! eof(file_handle))
            {
            bytes_read = read(file_handle, buffer,
                              sizeof(buffer));
            write(1, buffer, bytes_read);
            }
        }
}
```

Related Function: feof

execl

int **execl**(char *pathname*, char *arg0*, char *arg1*, ..., NULL);

Include file: <process.h>

Description:

execl executes the operating-system command specified by *pathname*
and passes a null-terminated list of command-line arguments.

The program that calls execl never resumes control.

execl does not support the PATH environment entry.

Example:

```
#include <process.h>
#include <stdio.h>

main()
{
    execl("DISKCOPY.COM", "DISKCOPY", "A:", "B:", NULL);
}
```

Related Functions: execle, execlp, execlpe

---

execle

int **execle**(char *pathname*, char *arg0*, ..., NULL, char *env[]*);

Include file: <process.h>

Description:

execle executes the operating-system command specified by *pathname* and passes a null-terminated list of command-line arguments as well as an array of pointers to environment entries.

The program that calls execle never resumes control.

execle does not support the PATH environment entry.

Example:

```
#include <process.h>
#include <stdio.h>

main()
{
    static char *env[] = {"A=TEST", "B=FILE", NULL};

    execle("TEST.EXE", "TEST", "ONE", "TWO", NULL, env);
}
```

Related Functions: execl, execlp, execlpe

---

execlp

int **execlp**(char *pathname*, char *arg0*, char *arg1*, ..., NULL);

Include file: <process.h>

Description:

execlp executes the operating-system command specified by *pathname* and passes a null-terminated list of command-line arguments.

execlp is identical to execl except that it supports the PATH environment entry.

The program that calls execlp never resumes control.

Example: See execl.

Related Functions: execl, execle, execlpe

---

execlpe

int **execlpe**(char *pathname*, char *arg0*, ..., NULL, char *env*[]);

Include file: <process.h>

Description:

execlpe executes the operating-system command specified by *pathname* and passes a null-terminated list of command-line arguments as well as an array of pointers to environment entries.

execlpe is identical to execle except that it supports the PATH environment entry.

The program that calls execlpe never resumes control.

Example: See execle.

Related Functions: execl, execle, execlp

---

execv

int **execv**(char *pathname*, char *argv*[]);

Include file: <process.h>

Description:

execv executes the operating-system command specified by *pathname* and passes an array of pointers to the command-line arguments.

execv is identical to execl except that it passes an array of pointers to the command-line arguments rather than a null-terminated list of arguments.

The program that calls execv never resumes control.

execv does not support the PATH environment entry.

Example:

```
#include <process.h>
#include <stdio.h>
```

(continued)

```
main()
{
    static char *args[] = {"TEST", "TEST.EXE", "A",
                                "B", "C", NULL};

    execv("TEST.EXE", args);
}
```

Related Functions: execve, execvp, execvpe

execve

int **execve**(char *pathname*, char *argv*[], char *env*[]);

Include file: <process.h>

Description:

execve executes the operating-system command specified by
pathname and passes an array of pointers to the command-line arguments as well as an array of pointers to environment entries.

execve is identical to execle except that it passes an array of pointers
to the command-line arguments rather than a null-terminated list of
arguments.

The program that executes execve never resumes control.

execve does not support the PATH environment entry.

Example:

```
#include <process.h>
#include <stdio.h>

main()
{
    static char *args[] = {"TEST", "TEST.EXE", "A",
                                "B", "C", NULL};
    static char *env[] = {"A=AAA", "B=BBB", NULL};

    execve("TEST.EXE", args, env);
}
```

Related Functions: execv, execvp, execvpe

execvp

int **execvp**(char *pathname*, char *argv*[]);

Include file: <process.h>

Description:

execvp executes the operating-system command specified by *pathname* and passes an array of pointers to the command-line arguments.

execvp is identical to execlp except that it passes an array of pointers to the command-line arguments rather than a null-terminated list of arguments.

The program that calls execvp never resumes control.

execvp supports the PATH environment entry.

Example: See execv.

Related Functions: execv, execve, execvpe

execvpe

int **execvpe**(char *pathname*, char *argv*[], char *env*[]);

Include file: <process.h>

Description:

execvpe executes the operating-system command specified by *pathname* and passes an array of pointers to the command-line arguments as well as an array of pointers to environment entries.

execvpe is identical to execlpe except that it passes an array of pointers to the command-line arguments rather than a null-terminated list of arguments.

The program that calls execvpe never resumes control.

execvpe supports the PATH environment entry.

Example: See execve.

Related Functions: execv, execve, execvp

exit

void **exit**(int *exit_status*);

Include file: <process.h> or <stdlib.h>

Description:

exit calls all exit-list routines defined by atexit, flushes file buffers, and closes files before ending the program. exit returns control to the operating system or calling process.

exit_status specifies the status value that the program returns to the operating system or the calling process. The DOS IF ERRORLEVEL batch command allows you to test the exit-status value.

Example:

```
#include <stdlib.h>
#include <stdio.h>

main()
{
    FILE *fp;

    if ((fp = fopen("TEST.DAT", "r")) == NULL)
        {
        printf("Error opening file\n");
        exit(1);
        }
    else
        /* statements*/
}
```

Related Functions: abort, atexit, _exit, onexit

_exit

_exit(int *exit_status*);

Include file: <stdlib.h>

Description:

_exit ends the current program and returns control to the operating system or calling process.

_exit is functionally similar to exit except that _exit does not call the exit-list routines defined by atexit.

Example: See exit.

Related Functions: abort, exit

---

exp

double **exp**(double *expression*);

Include file: <math.h>

Description:

exp returns the value of *e* raised to the value of the specified numeric expression.

If overflow occurs, exp returns the constant HUGE_VAL and sets the global variable *errno* to the value ERANGE.

Example:

```
#include <math.h>

main()
{
    double x;

    for (x = 0; x < 2; x += 0.1)
        printf("x = %f; exp(x) = %f\n", x, exp(x));
}
```

Related Functions: log, matherr, pow

_expand

void *_**expand**(void *_block*, size_t *desired_size*);

Include file: <malloc.h>

Description:

_expand changes the size of a previously allocated block of memory without moving the location of the block within the heap.

The realloc routine changes a block's size and, if necessary, location.

block is a pointer to the starting location of the block in memory.

desired_size specifies in bytes the desired size of the block.

If successful, _expand returns a pointer to the block. If insufficient memory exists, _expand returns NULL after it expands the block as much as possible.

Example:

```
#include <malloc.h>
#include <stdio.h>

main()
{
    char *block;

    if ((block = malloc(512)) == NULL)
        printf("Initial allocation failed\n");
    else if (_expand(block, 2048) == NULL)
        printf("Expansion failed\n");
    else
        printf("Allocation expanded as desired\n");
}
```

Related Functions: calloc, free, halloc, malloc, _msize, realloc

fabs

double **fabs**(double *expression*);

Include file: <math.h>

Description:

fabs returns the absolute value of a specified floating-point expression.

expression is the floating-point expression for which an absolute value will be returned.

Example:

```
#include <math.h>

main()
{
    float x;

    for (x = -1.0; x <= 1.0; x += 0.5)
        printf("x = %f; fabs(x) = %f\n", x, fabs(x));
}
```

Related Functions: abs, cabs, labs

fclose

int **fclose**(FILE *file_pointer);

Include file: <stdio.h>

Description:

fclose flushes the buffers associated with the specified file, closes the file, and updates the file's directory entry.

file_pointer is a file pointer associated with a file through the fopen function.

If successful, fclose returns the value 0. If an error occurs, such as an invalid file pointer, fclose returns the value EOF.

Example: See fopen.

Related Functions: fcloseall, fflush, fopen

fcloseall

int **fcloseall**(void);

Include file: <stdio.h>

Description:

fcloseall closes all open file streams except stdin, stdout, stderr, stdaux, and stdprn.

fcloseall flushes the buffers associated with all files opened by the fopen function and updates each file's directory entry.

If successful, fcloseall returns the value 0. If an error occurs, fcloseall returns the value EOF.

Example:

```
void error_handler(void)
{
    printf("Critical processing error\n");
    fcloseall();
    /* statements */
}
```

Related Functions: fclose, fflush, fopen, freopen

fcvt

char *__fcvt__(double *expression*, int *count*, int *__decimal_pos__, int *__sign__);

Include file: <stdlib.h>

Description:

fcvt converts a floating-point expression to a character-string representation, assigning only the digits to the string. fcvt returns the position for the decimal point but does not include the decimal point in the string.

expression is a floating-point expression to be converted to a character-string representation.

count specifies the number of digits to be included in the string.

decimal_pos is a pointer to an integer variable to which fcvt assigns the position of the decimal point.

sign is a pointer to an integer variable to which fcvt assigns the sign of the expression. If *sign* is 0, the expression is positive; otherwise, the expression is negative.

Example: See ecvt.

Related Functions: atof, atoi, atol, ecvt, gcvt

fdopen

FILE *__fdopen__(int *file_handle*, char *__file_type__);

Include file: <stdio.h>

Description:

fdopen associates a stream-file pointer with a file opened by the creat or open function for low-level file operations.

file_handle is a low-level file handle associated with a file through the creat or open function.

file_type is a character string that specifies how the program accesses the file. Characters and meanings are as follows:

Character	*Meaning*
r	opens the file for read access
w	opens the file for write access
a	opens the file for append operations

If you follow the character string with a plus sign (+), for example "r+", fdopen opens the file for read and write operations. If you include either a lowercase "b" or "t" following the file type, for example "rb", fdopen opens the file in binary or text mode, respectively.

If successful, fdopen returns a pointer to the file; otherwise, fdopen returns NULL.

Example:

```
#include <stdio.h>
#include <fcntl.h>

main()
{
    int file_handle;
    FILE *fp;

    if (file_handle = open("TEST.DAT", O_RDONLY) == -1)
        printf("Error opening TEST.DAT\n");
    else
        {
        /* statements */
        /* convert handle to stream */
        if ((fp = fdopen(file_handle, "r")) == NULL)
            printf("Error creating stream\n");
        else
            /* statements */
        }
}
```

Related Functions: fclose, fopen, freopen, open

feof

int **feof**(FILE *file_pointer);

Include file: <stdio.h>

Description:

feof returns true if a specified file has reached end-of-file (EOF).

file_pointer is a file pointer associated with a file through the fdopen, fopen, or freopen function.

If the file is at end-of-file, feof returns a nonzero value; otherwise, feof returns the value 0.

Example:

```
#include <stdio.h>
main(int argc, char *argv[])
{
    char buffer[256];
    FILE *fp;

    /* display file specified by argv[1] */
    if ((fp = fopen(argv[1], "r")) == NULL)
        printf("Error opening input file\n");
    else
        {
        while (! feof(fp))
            {
            fgets(buffer, sizeof(buffer), fp);
            fputs(buffer, stdout);
            }
        fclose(fp);
        }
}
```

Related Functions: eof, ferror, rewind

ferror

int **ferror**(FILE *file_pointer*);

Include file: <stdio.h>

Description:

ferror returns true if a specified file encounters an error in a read or write operation; otherwise, ferror returns false. If an error occurs, ferror continues to return true until you call an fclose, rewind, or clearerr function for the specified file.

file_pointer is a file pointer associated with a file through the fdopen, fopen, or freopen function.

Example:

```
#include <stdio.h>
```

(continued)

```
main(int argc, char *argv[])
{
    FILE *fp;
    char buffer[256];

    if ((fp = fopen(argv[1], "r")) == NULL)
        printf("Error opening the input file\n");
    else
        {
        while (! feof(fp))
            {
            fgets(buffer, sizeof(buffer), fp);
            fputs(buffer, stdout);
            if (ferror(fp))
                {
                printf("\07\07Error reading\n");
                clearerr(fp);
                }
            }
        fclose(fp);
        }
}
```

Related Functions: fclose, feof, rewind

fflush

int **fflush**(FILE *file_pointer);

Include file: <stdio.h>

Description:

fflush flushes the contents of a buffer for an output file or clears the contents of an input buffer.

file_pointer is a file pointer associated with a file through the fdopen, fopen, or freopen function.

If successful, fflush returns the value 0, otherwise, fflush returns the value EOF.

Related Functions: flushall, setbuf

_ffree

void **_ffree**(void far *buffer);

Include file: <malloc.h>

Description:

_ffree releases memory previously allocated from the far heap.

buffer is the starting address of a region in memory previously allocated by the _fmalloc function.

Example: See _fmalloc.

Related Functions: _fmalloc, free, _nfree

---

fgetc

int **fgetc**(FILE *file_pointer);

Include file: <stdio.h>

Description:

fgetc reads a character from the specified file, returns the character, and moves the file-position pointer to the next character in the file.

file_pointer is a file pointer associated with a file through the fdopen, fopen, or freopen function.

fgetc is functionally identical to getc except that fgetc is implemented as a function and getc is implemented as a macro.

If successful, fgetc returns the next character in the file. If an error or end-of-file occurs, fgetc returns the value EOF.

Example:

```
#include <stdio.h>

main(int argc, char *argv[])
{
    char letter;
    FILE *fp;

    if ((fp = fopen(argv[1], "r")) == NULL)
        printf("Error opening input file\n");
    else
        {
        while (! feof(fp))
            {
            letter = fgetc(fp);
            putchar(letter);
            }
        fclose(fp);
        }
}
```

Related Functions: fgetchar, getc, getchar

fgetchar

int **fgetchar**(void);

Include file: <stdio.h>

Description:

fgetchar reads and returns a character from stdin.

The fgetchar routine is functionally identical to getchar except that fgetchar is implemented as a function and getchar is implemented as a macro.

If successful, fgetchar returns a character. If an error or end-of-file occurs, fgetchar returns the value EOF.

Example:

```
#include <stdio.h>

main()
{
    char buffer[128];
    int i;

    printf("Type some characters and press Enter\n");
    for (i = 0; i < 127; i++)
        if ((buffer[i] = fgetchar()) == '\n')
            break;
    buffer[i] = NULL;
    printf("String entered: %s\n", buffer);
}
```

Related Functions: fgetc, getc, getchar

fgetpos

int **fgetpos**(FILE *file_pointer*, fpos_t *position*);

Include file: <stdio.h>

Description:

fgetpos returns the current value of a file-position pointer for use by the fsetpos function.

file_pointer is a file pointer associated with a file through the fdopen, fopen, or freopen function.

position is a pointer to a variable of type fpos_t (defined in stdio.h) to which fgetpos assigns the current file position.

If successful, fgetpos returns the value 0. If an error occurs, fgetpos returns a nonzero value and sets the global variable *errno* to one of the following values:

Value	Meaning
EINVAL	invalid argument
EBADF	invalid file pointer

Example:

```
#include <stdio.h>

main()
{
    FILE *fp;
    fpos_t position;
    char buffer[128];

    if ((fp = fopen("TEST.DAT", "rb")) == NULL)
        printf("Error opening TEST.DAT\n");
    else
        {
        fgets(buffer, sizeof(buffer), fp);
        fgetpos(fp, &position);   /* save position */
        fgets(buffer, sizeof(buffer), fp);
        /* statements */
        fsetpos(fp, &position);   /* restore position */
        /* statements */
        fclose(fp);
        }
}
```

Related Function: fsetpos

fgets

char ***fgets**(char *string*, int *max_char*, FILE *file_pointer*);

Include file: <stdio.h>

Description:

fgets reads a string of characters from the specified file and advances the file-position pointer.

fgets reads *maxchar*-1 characters or up to the first newline character. fgets assigns the NULL character to the position following the last character read.

string is the starting address of the buffer into which the characters are read.

max_char is an integer value that specifies the maximum number of characters to be read from the file.

file_pointer is a file pointer associated with a file through the fdopen, fopen, or freopen function.

If successful, fgets returns a pointer to the string of characters read. If an error or end-of-file occurs, fgets returns the value NULL.

Example: See fopen.

Related Functions: feof, fopen, fputs

_fheapchk

See _heapchk.

_fheapset

See _heapset.

fieeetomsbin

int **fieeetomsbin**(float *source*, float *target*);

Include file: <float.h> or <math.h>

Description:

fieeetomsbin converts a single-precision floating-point value stored in IEEE format to a value in Microsoft binary format for output to a random-access file.

Microsoft BASIC stores values in Microsoft binary format. If your program shares data files with a BASIC program, you might need to convert values from one format to another.

source is a pointer to a single-precision value in IEEE format.

target is a pointer to a single-precision value in Microsoft binary format.

If successful, fieeetomsbin returns the value 0. If overflow occurs, fieeetomsbin returns the value 1.

Related Functions: dieeetomsbin, dmsbintoieee, fmsbintoieee

filelength

long **filelength**(int *file_handle*);

Include file: <io.h>

Description:

filelength returns in bytes the size of the file associated with a speci-fied file handle.

file_handle is a file handle associated with a file through the open function.

If successful, filelength returns the number of bytes in the file. If an error occurs, filelength returns the value −1 and sets the global vari-able *errno* to the value EBADF.

Example:

```
#include <io.h>
#include <fcntl.h>

main(int argc, char *argv[])
{
    int file_handle;

    if ((file_handle = open(argv[1], O_RDONLY)) == -1)
        printf("Error opening input file\n");
    else
        {
        printf("%s is %ld bytes long\n",
                argv[1], filelength(file_handle));
        close(file_handle);
        }
}
```

fileno

int **fileno**(FILE *file_pointer);

Include file: <stdio.h>

Description:

fileno returns the current file handle associated with a specified file pointer.

file_pointer is a file pointer associated with a file through the fdopen, fopen, or freopen function. If the file pointer is invalid or nonexistent, fileno does not return an error-status value.

Example:

```
#include <stdio.h>

main(int argc, char *argv[])
{
    FILE *fp;
    long result;

    if ((fp = fopen(argv[1], "r")) == NULL)
        printf("Error opening input file\n");
    else
        {
        result = filelength(fileno(fp));
        printf("%s is %ld byteslong\n", argv[1], result);
        fclose(fp);
        }
}
```

Related Function: fopen

_floodfill

short far **_floodfill**(short x_loc, short y_loc, short boundary_color);

Include file: <graph.h>

Description:

_floodfill fills a graphics region on the screen using the current color and fill mask.

_floodfill fills a region bounded by the color *boundary_color*.

x_loc and *y_loc* specify the *x* and *y* coordinates of a point within the region to be filled.

Example:

```
#include <graph.h>
#include <stdio.h>

main()
{
    _setvideomode(_MRES16COLOR);
    _setcolor(3);
    _ellipse(_GBORDER, 10, 10, 100, 100);
    _setcolor(5);
    _floodfill(11, 11, 3);
    getchar();
    _setvideomode(_DEFAULTMODE);
}
```

Related Functions: _getfillmask, _setcolor, _setfillmask

floor

double **floor**(double *expression*);

Include file: <math.h>

Description:

floor returns a value that represents the largest whole number that is smaller than the specified floating-point value.

expression is the double-precision expression whose ''floor'' is to be returned.

Example:

```
#include <math.h>

main()
{
    double a = -99.5, b = 0.1, c = 10.7;
```

(continued)

```
    printf("%f becomes %f\n", a, floor(a));
    printf("%f becomes %f\n", b, floor(b));
    printf("%f becomes %f\n", c, floor(c));
}
```

This program produces the following result:

```
-99.500000 becomes -100.000000
0.100000 becomes 0.000000
10.700000 becomes 10.000000
```

Related Functions: ceil, fmod

flushall

int **flushall**(void);

Include file: <stdio.h>

Description:

flushall flushes all file buffers associated with open output files and clears all file buffers associated with open input files.

flushall does not close open files.

Related Functions: fclose, fcloseall, fflush

_fmalloc

See malloc.

fmod

double **fmod**(double *numerator*, double *denominator*);

Include file: <math.h>

Description:

fmod returns the floating-point remainder of a double-precision division operation.

If *denominator* is 0, fmod returns the value 0.

Example:

```
#include <math.h>

main()
{
    float a = 10.0, b = 1.5;

    printf("%f/%f yields a remainder of %f\n",
           a, b, fmod(a, b));
}
```

This program produces the following result:

```
10.000000/1.500000 yields a remainder of 1.000000
```

Related Functions: ceil, floor

---

fmsbintoieee

int **fmsbintoieee**(float *source*, float *target*);

Include file: <math.h>

Description:

fmsbintoieee converts a single-precision floating-point value stored in Microsoft binary format to a value in IEEE format.

source is a pointer to a single-precision value in Microsoft binary format.

target is a pointer to a single-precision value in IEEE format.

If successful, fmsbintoieee returns the value 0. If overflow occurs, fmsbintoieee returns the value 1.

Related Functions: dieeetomsbin, dmsbintoieee, fieeetomsbin

_fmsize

See _msize.

fopen

FILE *__fopen__(const char *_pathname_, const char *_access_mode_);

Include file: <stdio.h>

Description:

fopen opens the specified file and returns a file pointer to the file.

pathname is a character string that contains the complete path to the desired file.

_access_mode_ specifies how the program will use the file. Modes and meanings are as follows:

Mode	_Meaning_
r	opens the file for read access
w	opens the file for write access
a	opens the file for append access

If you follow the file-access-mode letter with a plus sign (+), for example ''r+'', the file is opened for read and write operations. If you include either a lowercase ''b'' or ''t'' following the file-access-mode letter, for example ''rb'', fopen opens the file in binary or text mode, respectively. If you don't specify either binary-mode or text-mode access, fopen uses the mode specified by the global variable __fmode_. Text mode is default.

If successful, fopen returns a file pointer to the file. If an error occurs, fopen returns the value NULL.

Example:

```
#include <stdio.h>

main(int argc, char *argv[])
{
    FILE *fp;
    char buffer[256];

    if ((fp = fopen(argv[1], "r")) == NULL)
        printf("Error opening input file\n");
    else
        {
        while (! feof(fp))
            {
            fgets(buffer, sizeof(buffer), fp);
```

(continued)

```
                    fputs(buffer, stdout);
                    }
            fclose(fp);
            }
}
```

Related Functions: fclose, fgets, fputs

FP_OFF

unsigned **FP_OFF**(char far *address*);

Include file: <dos.h>

Description:

FP_OFF returns the 16-bit offset portion of a 32-bit far pointer.

FP_OFF is a macro that works in conjunction with FP_SEG to divide a 32-bit far address into a 16-bit offset and segment.

Example:

```
#include <dos.h>

main()
{
    char far *a = 0xB8000001;
    void show_parts(char far *);

    show_parts(a);
}

void show_parts(char far *x)
{
    printf("Segment %x; offset %x\n",
            FP_SEG(x), FP_OFF(x));
}
```

Related Function: FP_SEG

FP_SEG

unsigned **FP_SEG**(char far *address*);

Include file: <stdio.h>

Description:

FP_SEG returns the 16-bit segment portion of a 32-bit far pointer.

FP_SEG is a macro that works in conjunction with FP_OFF to divide a 32-bit far address into a 16-bit offset and segment.

Example: See FP_OFF.

Related Function: FP_OFF

_fpreset

void **_fpreset**(void);

Include file: <float.h>

Description:

_fpreset reinitializes the floating-point-math package.

For MS-DOS versions prior to version 3.0, a call to exec, spawn, or system might alter the state of the math coprocessor. The _fpreset routine resets the coprocessor. Many programs use _fpreset to reset the coprocessor after a floating-point exception.

Example:

```
int handler(int signal, int number)
{
    /* statements */
    _fpreset();
}
```

Related Function: signal

fprintf

int **fprintf**(FILE *file_pointer*, const char *format_specifier*
        [, *argument*]...);

Include file: <stdio.h>

Description:

fprintf prints formatted data to the specified file.

fprintf is printf's counterpart for formatted file output.

file_pointer is a file pointer associated with an output file through the fdopen, fopen, or freopen function.

format_specifier is a character string that specifies the desired output format. See printf for more information about format specifiers.

*argument*s are optional expressions that fprintf outputs using the format specifications provided.

fprintf returns the number of characters written to the file.

Example:

```c
#include <stdio.h>

main()
{
    FILE *fp;
    int i;

    if ((fp = fopen("ASCII.DAT", "w")) == NULL)
        printf("Error opening ASCII.DAT\n");
    else
        {
        for (i = 0; i < 128; ++i)
            fprintf(fp, "%d\t%o\t%x\n", i, i, i);
        fclose(fp);
        }
}
```

Related Functions: fscanf, printf

fputc

int **fputc**(int *character*, FILE **file_pointer*);

Include file: <stdio.h>

Description:

fputc writes a character to a specified file.

character is a character to be written to a specified file.

file_pointer is a file pointer associated with the output file through the fdopen, fopen, or freopen function.

fputc is functionally identical to putc except that fputc is implemented as a function and putc is implemented as a macro.

If successful, fputc returns the character written; otherwise, it returns the value EOF.

Example:

```
#include <stdio.h>

main()
{
    FILE *fp;
    char letter;

    if ((fp = fopen("ALPHABET.DAT", "w")) == NULL)
        printf("Error opening ALPHABET.DAT\n");
    else
        {
        for (letter = 'A'; letter <= 'Z'; letter++)
            fputc(letter, fp);
        fclose(fp);
        }
}
```

Related Functions: fgetc, fputchar, putc

fputchar

int **fputchar**(int *character*);

Include file: <stdio.h>

Description:

fputchar writes a specified character to stdout.

character is an ASCII character to be sent to stdout.

fputchar is functionally identical to putchar except that fputchar is implemented as a function and putchar is implemented as a macro.

Example: See putchar.

Related Functions: fgetchar, fputc, putchar

fputs

int **fputs**(char *string*, FILE *file_pointer*);

Include file: <stdio.h>

Description:

fputs writes a null-terminated character string to a specified file.

string is a null-terminated character string to be written to a specified file.

file_pointer is a file pointer associated with an output file through the fdopen, fopen, or freopen function.

If successful, fputs returns the value 0. If an error occurs, fputs returns a nonzero value.

Example: See fopen.

Related Functions: fgets, puts

fread

size_t **fread**(void *buffer*, size_t *item_size*,
            size_t *num_items*, FILE *file_pointer*);

Include file: <stdio.h>

Description:

fread reads the specified number of items from a file.

fread enables you to quickly read arrays or other structures from a file.

buffer is a pointer to the start of a data buffer into which fread reads data.

item_size specifies in bytes the size of each item to be read.

num_items specifies the number of data items to be read from the file.

file_pointer is a file pointer associated with an input file through the fdopen, fopen, or freopen function.

fread returns a count of the number of items read.

Example:

```
#include <stdio.h>

main()
{
    int array[10];
    int i;
    FILE *fp;
```

(continued)

```
if ((fp = fopen("NUMBERS.DAT", "w")) == NULL)
    printf("Error opening NUMBERS.DAT\n");
else
    {
    for (i = 0; i < 10; ++i)
        fwrite(&i, sizeof(i), 1, fp);
    fclose(fp);
    if ((fp = fopen("NUMBERS.DAT", "r")) == NULL)
        printf("Error reopening NUMBERS.DAT\n");
    else
        {
        fread(array, sizeof(int), 10, fp);
        for (i = 0; i < 10; ++i)
            printf("%d\n", array[i]);
        fclose(fp);
        }
    }
}
```

Related Functions: fwrite, read

free

void **free**(void *buffer*);

Include file: <malloc.h> or <stdlib.h>

Description:

free releases memory previously allocated from the heap.

buffer is the starting address of a region of memory previously allocated from the heap by a calloc, malloc, or realloc function.

Example: See calloc.

Related Functions: calloc, _ffree, malloc, _nfree, realloc

_freect

unsigned int **_freect**(size_t *item_size*);

Include file: <malloc.h>

Description:

_freect returns the number of items of a specified size that can be allocated dynamically from memory.

item_size specifies in bytes the size of the item to be allocated.

Example:

```
#include <malloc.h>

main()
{
    printf("Number of ints: %u\n", _freect(sizeof(int)));
    printf("Number of floats: %u\n",
            _freect(sizeof(float)));
}
```

Related Functions: calloc, _expand, malloc, _memavl, _msize, realloc

freeopen

FILE *freopen(const char *pathname, const char *access_mode,
            FILE *file_pointer);

Include file: <stdio.h>

Description:

freopen closes the file currently associated with a file pointer and opens a second specified file, associating it with that file pointer.

pathname is a character string that contains the complete path to the desired file.

access_mode is a character string that specifies how the program is to access the file. See fopen for more information about mode specifiers.

file_pointer is a file pointer that freopen will associate with the new open file.

If successful, freopen returns a file pointer. If an error occurs, freopen returns the value NULL.

Example:

```
#include <stdio.h>
```

(continued)

```
main()
{
    /* route output for stdout to a file */
    int letter;
    FILE *fp;

    if ((freopen("STDOUT.DAT", "w", stdout)) == NULL)
        printf("Error redirecting stdout\n");
    else
        {
        for (letter = 'A'; letter <= 'Z'; letter++)
            putchar(letter);   /* written to file */
        fclose(fp);
        }
}
```

Related Functions: fclose, fopen

frexp

double **frexp**(double *expression*, int **exponent*);

Include file: <math.h>

Description:

frexp assigns the exponent of *expression* to the variable pointed to by *exponent* and returns the mantissa.

Example:

```
#include <math.h>

main()
{
    float x = 123.4567;
    int exponent;
    float mantissa;

    mantissa = frexp(x, &exponent);
    printf("Value %f; Mantissa %f; exponent %d\n",
            x, mantissa, exponent);
}
```

Related Function: ldexp

fscanf

int **fscanf**(FILE *file_pointer*, const char *format_specifier*
    [, *argument*]...);

Include file: <stdio.h>

Description:

fscanf reads formatted data from a specified file.

fscanf is scanf's counterpart for formatted file input.

file_pointer is a file pointer associated with the input file through the fdopen, fopen, or freopen function.

format_specifier is a character string that specifies the format of the data to be input. See scanf for more information about format specifiers.

*argument*s are the locations into which fprintf reads data using the format specifications provided.

If successful, fscanf returns a count of the number of variables assigned. If end-of-file occurs, fscanf returns the value EOF.

Example:

```
#include <stdio.h>

main()
{
    int i, a, b, c;
    FILE *fp;

    if ((fp = fopen("NUMBERS.DAT", "w")) == NULL)
        printf("Error opening NUMBERS.DAT\n");
    else
        {
        for (i = 0; i < 128; i++)
            fprintf(fp, "%d %o %x\n", i, i, i);
        fclose(fp);
        if ((fp = fopen("NUMBERS.DAT", "r")) == NULL)
            printf("Error reopening file\n");
        else
            {
            while (! feof(fp))
                {
                fscanf(fp, "%d %o %x", &a, &b, &c);
                printf("%d %o %x\n", a, b, c);
                }
            fclose(fp);
            }
        }
}
```

Related Functions: fprintf, scanf

fseek

int **fseek**(FILE *_file_pointer_, long _offset_, int _start_position_);

Include file: <stdio.h>

Description:

fseek allows you to move a file pointer to a specific offset for read and write operations.

_file_pointer_ is a file pointer associated with a file through the fdopen, fopen, or freopen function.

offset is a long-integer value that specifies the number of bytes to off-set the file pointer from the specified starting position.

_start_position_ is an integer value that specifies the location from which to offset. Values and corresponding meanings are as follows:

Value	_Meaning_
SEEK_SET	offsets from start of file
SEEK_CUR	offsets from current position
SEEK_END	offsets from end-of-file

If successful, fseek returns the value 0. If an error occurs, fseek returns a nonzero value.

Example:

```
#include <stdio.h>

main()
{
    FILE *fp;

    if ((fp = fopen("RANDOM.DAT", "w")) == NULL)
        printf("Error accessing RANDOM.DAT\n");
    else
        {
        fseek(fp, 0L, SEEK_END);   /* end-of-file */
        /* statements */
        fclose(fp);
        }
}
```

Related Functions: fgetpos, fsetpos, ftell

fsetpos

int **fsetpos**(FILE *file_pointer*, const fpos_t *position*);

Include file: <stdio.h>

Description:

fsetpos sets the file-pointer position to the location previously stored by fgetpos.

file_pointer is a file pointer associated with a file through the fdopen, fopen, or freopen function.

position is a file position previously stored by fgetpos.

If successful, fsetpos returns the value 0. If an error occurs, fsetpos returns a nonzero value and sets the global variable *errno* to one of the following values:

Value	Meaning
EINVAL	invalid argument
EBADF	invalid file pointer

Example: See fgetpos.

Related Functions: fgetpos, fseek

fstat

int **fstat**(int *file_handle*, struct stat *fileinfo*);

Include files: <sys\types.h> and <sys\stat.h>

Description:

fstat returns specifics about a file associated with a specified file handle.

file_handle is a file handle associated with a file through the creat or open function.

fileinfo is a pointer to a structure defined in sys\stat.h as follows:

```
struct stat
    {
    dev_t st_dev;       /* number of drive containing file */
    ino_t st_ino;               /* not used by MS-DOS */
    unsigned short st_mode;  /* file mode */
    short st_nlink;          /* always 1 */
    short uid;               /* not used by MS-DOS */
    short gid;               /* not used by MS-DOS */
    dev_t st_rdev;           /* same as st_dev */
    off_t st_size;           /* file size in bytes */
    time_t st_atime;         /* last modification date */
    time_t st_mtime;         /* same as st_atime */
    time_t st_ctime;         /* same as st_atime */
    };
```

If successful, fstat returns the value 0. If an error occurs, fstat returns the value −1 and sets the global variable *errno* to the value EBADF.

Example:

```
#include <fcntl.h>
#include <sys\types.h>
#include <sys\stat.h>

main(int argc, char *argv[])
{
    int file_handle;
    struct stat fileinfo;

    if ((file_handle = open(argv[1], O_RDONLY)) == 1)
        printf("Error opening %s\n", argv[1]);
    else
        {
        fstat(file_handle, &fileinfo);
        printf("%s %ld\n", argv[1], fileinfo.st_size);
        close(file_handle);
        }
}
```

Related Functions: access, chmod, filelength, stat

---

ftell

long **ftell**(FILE *file_pointer*);

Include file: <stdio.h>

Description:

ftell returns the current position of a file pointer within a file.

file_pointer is a file pointer associated with a file through the fdopen, fopen, or freopen function.

If successful, ftell returns the current offset of the file pointer. If an error occurs, ftell returns the value −1 and sets the global variable *errno* to one of the following values:

Value	Meaning
EBADF	invalid file pointer
EINVAL	invalid argument

Example:

```
#include <stdio.h>

main(int argc, char *argv[])
{
    FILE *fp;
    char buffer[128];

    if ((fp = fopen(argv[1], "r")) == NULL)
        printf("Error accessing %s\n", argv[1]);
    else
        {
        while (! feof(fp))
            {
            /* display offset of each line */
            printf("%ld\n", ftell(fp));
            fgets(buffer, sizeof(buffer), fp);
            }
        fclose(fp);
        }
}
```

Related Functions: fseek, lseek

ftime

void **ftime**(struct timeb *time*);

Include files: <sys\types.h> and <sys\timeb.h>

Description:

ftime returns the current time.

time is a pointer to a structure of type timeb defined in the include file timeb.h as follows:

```
struct timeb
    {
    time_t time;        /* seconds since 01/01/1970 */
    unsigned short millitm;  /* milliseconds */
    short timezone;     /* difference between GMT
                           and local time in minutes */
    short dstflag;      /* nonzero if daylight saving time */
    };
```

Example:

```
#include <sys\types.h>
#include <sys\timeb.h>
#include <time.h>

main()
{
    struct timeb time;
    char *cur_time;

    ftime(&time);
    cur_time = ctime(&(time.time));
    printf("%s\n", cur_time);
}
```

This program produces the following result:

```
Mon Jan 15 13:17:12 1990
```

Related Functions: asctime, ctime, gmtime, localtime, time, tzset

fwrite

size_t **fwrite**(const void *buffer*, size_t *item_size*,
            size_t *num_items*, FILE *file_pointer*);

Include file: <stdio.h>

Description:

fwrite writes a specified number of items to a file.

fwrite enables you to write arrays or other data structures to a file.

buffer is the starting address of the data to be written.

item_size specifies in bytes the size of individual data items.

num_items specifies the number of items to be written to the file.

file_pointer is a file pointer associated with an output file through the
fdopen, fopen, or freopen function.

If successful, fwrite returns the number of items actually written to the file.

Example: See fread.

Related Functions: fread, write

gcvt

char *__gcvt__(double *expression*, int *num_digits*, char *__buffer__);

Include file: <stdlib.h>

Description:

gcvt converts a floating-point expression to a character string.

expression is a double-precision expression to be converted to a character string.

num_digits specifies the number of digits to be stored.

buffer is a pointer to the character string in which the converted value is to be stored.

Unlike ecvt and fcvt, gcvt stores the decimal point in the character string.

Example:

```
#include <stdlib.h>

main()
{
    char buffer[128];

    gcvt(123.4567, 8, buffer);
    printf("%s\n", buffer);
}
```

Related Functions: ecvt, fcvt

_getbkcolor

long far **_getbkcolor**(void);

Include file: <graph.h>

Description:

_getbkcolor returns the current graphics background color.

Example:

```
#include <graph.h>

void draw_box(void)
{
    long save_color;

    save_color = _getbkcolor();
    _setbkcolor(5L);
    /* statements */
    _setbkcolor(save_color);
}
```

Related Function: _setbkcolor

getc

int **getc**(FILE *file_pointer);

Include file: <stdio.h>

Description:

getc reads a character from a specified file and advances the file pointer to the next character.

file_pointer is a file pointer associated with the input file through the fdopen, fopen, or freopen function.

getc is functionally identical to fgetc except that getc is implemented as a macro and fgetc is implemented as a function.

If successful, getc returns the next letter in the file. If end-of-file occurs, getc returns the value EOF.

Example:

```
#include <stdio.h>

main(int argc, char *argv[])
{
    FILE *fp;
    int letter;

    if ((fp = fopen(argv[1], "r")) == NULL)
        printf("Error opening %s\n", argv[1]);
```

(continued)

```
else
    {
    while (! feof(fp))
        {
        letter = getc(fp);
        putchar(letter);
        }
    fclose(fp);
    }
}
```

Related Functions: fgetc, getchar, putc, putchar

getch

int **getch**(void);

Include file: <conio.h>

Description:

getch reads a character from the keyboard without echoing the character to the screen.

If the user presses a function key or an arrow key, getch returns the value 0. Your program must call getch a second time to determine the scan code.

Example:

```
#include <conio.h>
#include <stdio.h>

main()
{
    char password[128];
    int i;

    printf("Type a 10-letter password\n");
    for (i = 0; i < 10; i++)
        password[i] = getch();
    password[i] = NULL;
    printf("Password is %s\n", password);
}
```

Related Functions: getchar, getche, putch

getchar

int **getchar**(void);

Include file: <stdio.h>

Description:

getchar reads a character from stdin.

getchar is functionally identical to fgetchar except that getchar is implemented as a macro and fgetchar is implemented as a function.

If successful, getchar returns a character from stdin. If end-of-file occurs, getchar returns the value EOF.

Example:

```
#include <stdio.h>

main()
{
    int letter;

    printf("Type a line and press Enter\n");
    while ((letter = getchar()) != '\n')
        putchar(letter);
}
```

Related Functions: fgetchar, getc, putchar

getche

int **getche**(void);

Include file: <conio.h>

Description:

getche reads a character from the keyboard and echoes the character to the screen.

If the user presses a function key or an arrow key, getche returns the value 0. Your program must call getche a second time to determine the scan code.

Example: See getch.

Related Functions: getch, getchar, putch

_getcolor

short far **_getcolor**(void);

Include file: <graph.h>

Description:

_getcolor returns the current graphics pixel color.

Example:

```
#include <graph.h>

void draw_box(void)
{
    short save_color;

    save_color = _getcolor();
    _setcolor(5);
    /* statements */
    _setcolor(save_color);
}
```

Related Function: _setcolor

_getcurrentposition

struct xycoord far **_getcurrentposition**(void);

Include file: <graph.h>

Description:

_getcurrentposition returns the logical coordinates of the current graphics position.

The include file graph.h defines the structure xycoord as follows:

```
struct xycoord
    {
    short xcoord;
    short ycoord;
    };
```

Example:

```
#include <graph.h>
```

(continued)

```
main ()
{
    struct xycoord position;

    _setvideomode (_MRES16COLOR) ;
    position = _getcurrentposition () ;
    /* statements */
    _setvideomode (_DEFAULTMODE) ;
}
```

Related Function: _gettextposition

getcwd

char *getcwd(char *pathname, int max_char);

Include file: <direct.h>

Description:

getcwd returns the current directory.

pathname is a character string buffer to which getcwd assigns the current directory.

max_char is an integer value that specifies the number of characters in the directory name. MS-DOS supports pathnames of up to 64 characters.

getcwd allocates the specified number of bytes for the directory name. You can release this memory by using the free function.

If successful, getcwd returns a pointer to the directory name. If an error occurs, getcwd returns the value NULL and sets the global variable *errno* to one of the following values:

Value	Meaning
ENOMEM	insufficient memory for getcwd to allocate space for the directory name.
ERANGE	path name longer than *max_char* characters

Example:

```
#include <direct.h>

main ()
{
    char *directory[64];
```

(continued)

```
    getcwd(directory[1], 64);
    printf("Current directory is %s\n", directory[1]);
    free(directory);   /* release allocated memory */
}
```

Related Functions: chdir, mkdir, rmdir

getenv

char *getenv(const char *variable_name);

Include file: <stdlib.h>

Description:

getenv returns a pointer to the character string containing the value of an environment entry. If the entry does not exist, getenv returns the value NULL.

Example:

```
#include <stdlib.h>

main()
{
    char *entry;

    entry = malloc(128);
    entry = getenv("PATH");
    if (*entry)
        printf("PATH = %s\n", entry);
    else
        printf("PATH not defined\n");
}
```

This program produces the following result:

PATH = C:\DOS;C:\RBIN;C:\MSC

Related Function: putenv

_getfillmask

unsigned char far * far _getfillmask(unsigned char far *mask);

Include file: <graph.h>

Description:

_getfillmask returns the 8×8-pixel bit mask used for graphics fill operations.

The fill mask is an 8×8 array of bits that specifies whether a pixel is turned on or off in the fill pattern.

If no fill mask is set, _getfillmask returns the value NULL.

Example: See _setfillmask.

Related Functions: _floodfill, _setfillmask

_getimage

void far _**getimage**(short *xleft*, short *ytop*, short *xright*,
          short *ybottom*, char far *image_buffer*);

Include file: <graph.h>

Description:

_getimage stores a screen image bounded by the specified rectangle. The coordinates (*xleft*, *ytop*) and (*xright*, *ybottom*) specify the coordinates of the bounding rectangle.

image_buffer is a pointer to the start of the buffer that stores the image. You can use the _imagesize function to determine the number of bytes needed for the buffer.

Example: See _putimage.

Related Functions: _imagesize, _putimage

_getlinestyle

unsigned short far _**getlinestyle**(void);

Include file: <graph.h>

Description:

_getlinestyle returns a bit mask that specifies the line style used by routines such as _lineto.

The line style is a 16-bit mask that specifies which pixels are turned on. By turning on and off various pixels, you can change the style of lines drawn in graphics operations.

If no line style has been selected, _getlinestyle returns the default style.

Example: See _setlinestyle.

Related Functions: _lineto, _rectangle, _setlinestyle

_getlogcoord

See _getviewcoord.

_getphyscoord

struct xycoord far **_getphyscoord**(short *x_view*, short *y_view*);

Include file: <graph.h>

Description:

_getphyscoord translates logical graphics coordinates into physical device coordinates.

x_view and *y_view* are the view coordinates to be translated into physical coordinates. Also see _getviewcoord.

Example:

```
#include <graph.h>

main()
{
    struct xycoord loc;

    _setvideomode(_MRES16COLOR);
    _setvieworg(50, 50);
    loc = _getphyscoord(10, 10);
    /* statements */
    _setvideomode(_DEFAULTMODE);
}
```

Related Functions: _getviewcoord, _setvieworg

getpid

int **getpid**(void);

Include file: <process.h>

Description:

getpid returns the process ID (PID) for the current process.

The process ID is unique for each process.

Example:

```
#include <process.h>

main()
{
    printf("Process ID is %d\n", getpid());
}
```

This program produces the following result:

```
Process ID is 2820
```

_getpixel

short far **_getpixel**(short *xloc*, short *yloc*);

Include file: <graph.h>

Description:

_getpixel returns the pixel value at the specified coordinates.

The pixel value returned is dependent upon the current video mode and palette.

xloc and *yloc* specify the coordinates of the desired pixel. If the coordinates are outside the clip region or the program is not in a graphics mode, _getpixel returns the value −1.

Related Functions: _setpixel, _setvideomode

gets

char ***gets**(char *string*);

Include file: <stdio.h>

Description:

gets reads a line of input from stdin.

string is the character string to which the characters are assigned.

gets reads characters up to the first newline character and replaces the newline character with the NULL character.

If successful, gets returns a pointer to the string read. If an error or end-of-file occurs, gets returns the value NULL.

Example:

```
#include <stdio.h>

main()
{
    char str[128];

    puts("Type a line and press Enter");
    gets(str);
    puts(str);
}
```

Related Functions: fgets, puts

_gettextcolor

short far *_gettextcolor(void);

Include file: <graph.h>

Description:

_gettextcolor returns the current text color used by the _outtext function.

The _settextcolor routine allows you to specify a color for text display.

Example: See _settextcolor.

Related Functions: _outtext, _settextcolor

_gettextposition

struct rccoord far _gettextposition(void);

Include file: <graph.h>

Description:

_gettextposition returns the current row and column position used for text output by _outtext.

The _settextposition routine allows you to specify the row and column position for text output by the _outtext function.

The include file graph.h defines the structure rccoord as follows:

```
struct rccoord
    {
    short row;
    short col;
    };
```

Example:

```
#include <graph.h>

main()
{
    struct rccoord position, save_position;

    save_position = _gettextposition();
    position.row = 10;
    position.col = 10;
    _settextposition(position.row, position.col);
    _outtext("Test message");
    _settextposition(save_position.row,
                     save_position.col);
    /* statements */
}
```

Related Function: _settextposition

_getvideoconfig

struct videoconfig far * far _**getvideoconfig**(struct videoconfig
                                            far *_configuration_);

Include file: <graph.h>

Description:

_getvideoconfig returns the current video environment.

The include file graph.h defines the structure videoconfig as follows:

```
struct videoconfig
    {
    short numxpixels;
    short numypixels;
    short numtextcols;
    short numtextrows;
    short numcolors;
    short bitsperpixel;
    short numvideopages;
    short mode;
    short adapter;
    short monitor;
    short memory;
    };
```

Example:

```
#include <graph.h>

main()
{
    struct videoconfig video;

    _getvideoconfig(&video);
    printf("X pixels: %d\tY pixels: %d\n",
            video.numxpixels, video.numypixels);
    printf("Text rows: %d\tText columns: %d\n",
            video.numtextrows, video.numtextcols);
    printf("Colors: %d\tPages: %d\tBits per pixel: %d\n",
            video.numcolors, video.numvideopages,
            video.bitsperpixel);
}
```

Related Function: _setvideomode

_getviewcoord

struct xycoord far **_getviewcoord**(short *x_physical*, short *y_physical*);

Include file: <graph.h>

Description:

_getviewcoord translates physical device coordinates into view coordinates.

The _setvieworg routine defines the view coordinates for graphics operations.

The include file graph.h defines the structure xycoord as follows:

```
struct xycoord
    {
    short xcoord;
    short ycoord;
    };
```

x_physical and *y_physical* are the physical device coordinates to be translated into view coordinates.

Example:

```
#include <graph.h>

main()
{
    struct xycoord loc;

    _setvideomode(_MRES16COLOR);
    _setvieworg(100, 100);
    loc = _getviewcoord(115, 125);
    /* statements */
    _setvideomode(_DEFAULTMODE);
}
```

Related Functions: _getphyscoord, _setvieworg

_getw

int **getw**(FILE *file_pointer*);

Include file: <stdio.h>

Description:

_getw returns an integer value from a file and advances the file pointer to the next position.

Because the numeric value for EOF is a valid integer, you should use the routine feof to determine whether getw has encountered end-of-file.

Example:

```
#include <stdio.h>
```

(continued)

```
main()
{
    int i;
    FILE *fp;

    if ((fp = fopen("NUMBERS.DAT", "wb")) == NULL)
        printf("Error opening NUMBERS.DAT\n");
    else
        {
        for (i = 0; i < 100; ++i)
            putw(i, fp);
        fclose(fp);
        if ((fp = fopen("NUMBERS.DAT", "rb")) == NULL)
            fprintf(fp, "Error accessing NUMBERS.DAT\n");
        else
            {
            while (! feof(fp))
                printf("%d\n", getw(fp));
            fclose(fp);
            }
        }
}
```

Related Functions: feof, putw

gmtime

struct tm ***gmtime**(const time_t *time*);

Include file: <time.h>

Description:

gmtime returns the current Greenwich mean time.

The include file time.h defines the structure tm as follows:

```
struct tm
    {
    int tm_sec;    /* seconds (0 through 59) */
    int tm_min;    /* minutes (0 through 59) */
    int tm_hour;   /* hours (0 through 23) */
    int tm_mday;   /* days (1 through 31) */
    int tm_mon;    /* months since January */
    int tm_year;   /* years since 1900 */
    int tm_wday;   /* days since Sunday */
    int tm_yday;   /* days since January 1 */
    int tm_isdt;   /* always 0 for GMT */
    };
```

time is a pointer to a long-integer value that contains the number of seconds since midnight, 01/01/1970, and is returned by the time routine.

Example:

```
#include <time.h>

main()
{
    time_t seconds;
    struct tm *gm;

    time(&seconds);
    gm = gmtime(&seconds);
    printf("Greenwich mean time: %s\n", asctime(gm));
}
```

Related Functions: asctime, ctime, ftime, localtime, time

halloc

void huge *__halloc__(long *num_elements*, size_t *element_size*);

Include file: <malloc.h>

Description:

halloc allocates memory for huge arrays and initializes each element in the array to 0. If the array size exceeds 128 KB, the size of each array element must be a power of 2.

If successful, halloc returns a pointer to the allocated memory. If an error occurs, halloc returns the value NULL.

Example:

```
#include <malloc.h>
#include <stdio.h>

main()
{
    int huge *array;
    long int i;

    if ((array = halloc(100000L, sizeof(int))) == NULL)
        printf("Memory allocation failed\n");
    else
        {
        for (i = 0; i < 100000L; ++i)
            array[i] = i;
        /* statements */
        hfree(array);
        }
}
```

Related Function: hfree

_harderr

void **_harderr**(void(far *_handler_)());

Include file: <dos.h>

Description:

_harderr installs a user-defined function that serves as an INT 0x24 critical-error handler.

By default, the DOS critical-error handler displays the message

```
Abort, Retry, Fail?
```

If an error occurs, the handler is called with the following parameters:

```
handler(unsigned device_error, unsigned error_code,
        unsigned far *device_header);
```

For more information about critical-error handlers, see _Advanced MS-DOS Programming, 2nd ed._, by Ray Duncan, and my _Microsoft C: Secrets, Shortcuts, and Solutions_, both published by Microsoft Press.

Example:

```
#include <dos.h>
#include <stdio.h>

unsigned int critical_error;   /* global critical-
                                  error flag */
main()
{
    FILE *fp;
    void far error_handler(unsigned, unsigned,
                           unsigned far *);

    _harderr(error_handler); /* install critical-
                                error handler */
    do
        {
        critical_error = 0;
        if (!(fp = fopen("A:TEST", "r")))
            {
            if (! critical_error)
                puts("Error opening TEST");
            else
                {
                if (critical_error == _HARDERR_ABORT)
                    exit(3);
                else if (critical_error == _HARDERR_FAIL)
```

(continued)

120

```
                    break;    /* continue without
                                 opening file */
                }
            }
        else
            {
            puts("TEST successfully opened");
            fclose(fp);
            }
        }
    while (critical_error != 0);
}

#include <bios.h>
#include <ctype.h>

void far error_handler(unsigned int ax, unsigned int di,
                        unsigned far *header)
{
    int done = 0;
    char response;

    printf("\nInsert disk in drive or turn on printer");
    critical_error = 1;    /* set critical-error
                               flag to true */
    while (! done)
        {
        printf("\nAbort, Retry, Fail? ");
        response = _bios_keybrd(_KEYBRD_READ);
        switch (_toupper(response))
            {
            case 'A': critical_error = _HARDERR_ABORT;
                      done = 1;
                      break;
            case 'R': critical_error = _HARDERR_RETRY;
                      done = 1;
                      break;
            case 'F': critical_error = _HARDERR_FAIL;
                      done = 1;
                      break;
            };
        }
    _hardretn(0);
}
```

Related Functions: _hardresume, _hardretn

_hardresume

void **_hardresume**(int *status*);

Include file: <dos.h>

Description:

_hardresume returns control to MS-DOS from a user-defined critical-error handler installed by using the _harderr function.

status is an integer value that directs MS-DOS to take the appropriate action. Values and corresponding actions are as follows:

Value	*Action*
_HARDERR_ABORT	abort the current program
_HARDERR_FAIL	fail the system service causing the error
_HARDERR_IGNORE	ignore the error
_HARDERR_RETRY	retry the operation causing the error

Example: See _harderr.

Related Functions: _harderr, _hardretn

_hardretn

void **_hardretn**(int *error*);

Include file: <dos.h>

Description:

_hardretn returns control from a user-defined critical-error handler installed by using the _harderr function to the program causing the error.

_hardretn returns control to the program at the line following the error-causing line.

Example: See _harderr.

Related Functions: _harderr, _hardresume

_heapchk, _fheapchk, _nheapchk

int **_heapchk**(void);

or

int **_fheapchk**(void);

or

int **_nheapchk**(void);

Include file: <malloc.h>

Description:

_heapchk returns information about the default heap; _fheapchk returns information about the far heap; and _nheapchk returns information about the near heap.

The returned value represents the heap status. Values and corresponding meanings are as follows:

Value	*Meaning*
_HEAPBADBEGIN	bad initial header information
_HEAPBADNODE	damaged node in the heap
_HEAPEMPTY	heap is uninitialized
_HEAPOK	heap is consistent

Example:

```
#include <malloc.h>
#include <stdio.h>

main()
{
    int *array;

    if ((array = malloc(1000)) == NULL)
        printf("Memory could not be allocated\n");
    else
        {
        switch (_heapchk())
            {
            case _HEAPBADBEGIN: printf("Bad header\n");
                                break;
            case _HEAPBADNODE:  printf("Bad node\n");
                                break;
            case _HEAPEMPTY:    printf("Empty\n");
                                break;
            case _HEAPOK:       printf("Heap OK\n");
                                break;
            }
        free(array);
        }
}
```

Related Functions: _fheapset, _fheapwalk, _heapset, _heapwalk, _nheapset, _nheapwalk

_heapset, _fheapset, _nheapset

int **_heapset**(unsigned int *heap_value*);

or

int **_fheapset**(unsigned int *heap_value*);

or

int **_nheapset**(unsigned int *heap_value*);

Include file: <malloc.h>

Description:

_heapset, _fheapset, and _nheapset initialize the heap to the specified value and perform a heap consistency check.

heap_value is a value to be assigned to each heap location.

_heapset, _fheapset, and _nheapset return the same values as the _heapchk function.

Related Functions: _fheapchk, _fheapwalk, _heapchk, _heapwalk, _nheapchk, _nheapwalk

_heapwalk, _fheapwalk, _nheapwalk

int **_heapwalk**(struct _heapinfo *_heap_entry_*);

or

int **_fheapwalk**(struct _heapinfo *_heap_entry_*);

or

int **_nheapwalk**(struct _heapinfo *_heap_entry_*);

Include file: <malloc.h>

Description:

_heapwalk, _fheapwalk, and _nheapwalk traverse the nodes of the heap and return status information about the nodes.

_heapwalk traverses the default heap one node at a time and returns specific information about each node. _fheapwalk does the same for the far heap; _nheapwalk does the same for the near heap. The include file malloc.h defines the structure _heapinfo as follows:

```
struct _heapinfo
    {
    int far *_pentry;   /*entry pointer */
    size_t _size;       /*size in bytes */
    int _useflag;
    };
```

_heapwalk returns the same consistency-check values as _heapchk.
_heapwalk also returns the value _HEAPEND, which indicates when
you reach end of the heap, and the value _HEAPBADPTTC, which
indicates an invalid pointer in the _pentry member.

To start the walk, pass to _heapwalk a structure that has the member
_pentry set to NULL.

The _useflag member will equal the value _USEDENTRY if the entry
is in use; otherwise, the _useflag member will equal the value
_FREEENTRY.

Example:

```
#include <malloc.h>
#include <stdio.h>

main()
{
    struct _heapinfo hinfo;
    int *a, *b;

    a = malloc(50);
    b = malloc(100);
    if ((*a && *b) == NULL)
        printf("Error allocating memory\n");
    else
        {
        hinfo._pentry = NULL;
        while (_heapwalk(&hinfo) == _HEAPOK)
            printf("Location %p; size %u; %s\n",
                    hinfo._pentry, hinfo._size,
                    (hinfo._useflag == _USEDENTRY)
                    ? "used" : "free");
        free(a);
        free(b);
        }
}
```

This program produces the following output:

```
Location 2C07:124A; size 50; used
Location 2C07:127E; size 100; used
Location 2C07:12E4; size 3354; free
```

Related Functions: _fheapchk, _fheapset, _heapchk, _heapset,
_nheapchk, _nheapset

hfree

void **hfree**(void huge *array*);

Include file: <malloc.h>

Description:

hfree releases memory allocated for a huge array through the halloc function.

array is a huge array previously allocated through the halloc function.

Example: See halloc.

Related Functions: free, halloc

hypot

double **hypot**(double *x*, double *y*);

Include file: <math.h>

Description:

hypot returns the length of the hypotenuse of a right triangle.

If overflow occurs, hypot returns the value HUGE_VAL and sets the global variable *errno* to the value ERANGE.

Example:

```
#include <math.h>

main()
{
    printf("x = %f; y = %f; z = %f\n", 3.0, 4.0,
            hypot(3.0, 4.0));
}
```

This program produces the following result:

```
x = 3.000000; y = 4.000000; z = 5.000000
```

_imagesize

long far **_imagesize**(short *xleft*, short *ytop*, short *xright*,
short *ybottom*);

Include file: <graph.h>

Description:

_imagesize returns the number of bytes needed to store an image that
is bounded by the specified rectangle.

The value returned by _imagesize is dependent upon the number of
bits per pixel and the current video configuration.

Example: See _putimage.

Related Functions: _getimage, _putimage

inp

int **inp**(unsigned int *port*);

Include file: <conio.h>

Description:

inp reads a byte value from the specified port.

port is the desired port address in the range 0 through 65,535.

Example:

```
#include <conio.h>
#include <stdio.h>

main()
{
    int speaker_value;

    speaker_value = inp(97);
    outp(97, speaker_value + 3);
    getchar();
    outp(97, speaker_value);
}
```

Related Functions: outp, outpw

int86

int **int86**(int *interrupt_number*, union REGS **inregs*,
　　　union REGS **outregs*);

Include file: <dos.h>

Description:

int86 executes the specified 8086-family interrupt.

interrupt_number is an integer value that specifies the 8086 service to
be performed. For more information about 8086 interrupts, see *IBM
ROM BIOS: Programmer's Quick Reference* by Ray Duncan, published
by Microsoft Press.

The include file dos.h defines the union REGS. See intdos.

int86 returns the value of the AX register when the specified service
completes execution.

inregs points to the register values to be sent to the service. *outregs*
points to the register values after the service completes.

Example:

```
#include <dos.h>

main()
{
    union REGS inregs, outregs;

    /* print the screen */
    int86(5, &inregs, &outregs);
}
```

Related Functions: int86x, intdos

int86x

int **int86x**(int *interrupt_number*, union REGS **inregs*,
　　　union REGS **outregs*, struct SREGS **segregs*);

Include file: <dos.h>

Description:

int86x executes the specified 8086-family interrupt and provides support for the segment registers CS, DS, SS, and ES.

int86x is functionally identical to int86 except that int86x supports the segment registers.

The include file dos.h defines the union REGS. See intdos.

segregs is a pointer to a structure containing the segment registers. See intdosx.

Example: See int86.

Related Functions: int86, intdosx

---

intdos

int **intdos**(union REGS *inregs*, union REGS *outregs*);

Include file: <dos.h>

Description:

intdos calls a DOS service by using interrupt 0x21.

For more information about the DOS services, see *MS-DOS Functions: Programmer's Quick Reference* by Ray Duncan, published by Microsoft Press.

The include file dos.h defines the union REGS as follows:

```
struct WORDREGS
    {
    unsigned int ax;
    unsigned int bx;
    unsigned int cx;
    unsigned int dx;
    unsigned int si;
    unsigned int di;
    unsigned int cflag;
    };

struct BYTEREGS
    {
    unsigned char al, ah;
    unsigned char bl, bh;
    unsigned char cl, ch;
    unsigned char dl, dh;
    };

union REGS
    {
    struct WORDREGS x;
    struct BYTEREGS h;
    };
```

intdos returns the value of the AX register when the specified service completes execution.

Example:

```
#include <dos.h>

main()
{
    /* display DOS version number */
    union REGS inregs, outregs;

    inregs.h.ah = 0x30;
    intdos(&inregs, &outregs);
    printf("DOS version number %d.%d\n",
            outregs.h.al, outregs.h.ah);
}
```

Related Functions: int86, intdosx

intdosx

int **intdosx**(union REGS *inregs*, union REGS *outregs*,
            struct SREGS *segregs*);

Include file: <dos.h>

Description:

intdosx calls a DOS service by using interrupt 0x21 and provides support for the segment registers ES, CS, SS, and DS.

intdosx is functionally identical to intdos except that intdosx supports the segment registers.

segregs is a pointer to a structure containing the segment registers defined in the include file dos.h as follows:

```
struct SREGS
    {
    unsigned int es;
    unsigned int cs;
    unsigned int ss;
    unsigned int ds;
    };
```

Example: See intdos.

Related Functions: int86x, intdos

isalnum

int **isalnum**(int *character*);

Include file: <ctype.h>

Description:

isalnum returns a nonzero value if the specified character is in the range "A" through "Z," "a" through "z," or "0" through "9."

character is the ASCII character to be tested.

Example:

```
if (isalnum(letter))
    /* statement */
```

Related Functions: isalpha, isascii, iscntrl, isdigit, isgraph, islower, isprint, ispunct, isspace, isupper, isxdigit

isalpha

int **isalpha**(int *character*);

Include file: <ctype.h>

Description:

isalpha returns a nonzero value if the specified character is in the range "A" through "Z" or "a" through "z."

character is the ASCII character to be tested.

Example:

```
if (isalpha(letter))
    /* statement */
```

Related Functions: isalnum, isascii, iscntrl, isdigit, isgraph, islower, isprint, ispunct, isspace, issupper, isxdigit

isascii

int **isascii**(int *character*);

Include file: <ctype.h>

Description:

isascii returns a nonzero value if the specified character is an ASCII character in the range 0 through 127.

character is the value to be tested.

Example:

```
if (isascii(letter))
    /* statement */
```

Related Functions: isalnum, isalpha, iscntrl, isdigit, isgraph, islower, isprint, ispunct, isspace, isupper, isxdigit

isatty

int **isatty**(int *file_handle*);

Include file: <io.h>

Description:

isatty returns a nonzero value if the specified handle is associated with a device or the value 0 if the handle is associated with a file.

file_handle is a file handle associated with a device or file through the open function.

Example:

```
if (isatty(fileno(stdin)))
    printf("Device input\n");
else
    printf("File input\n");
```

Related Function: fileno

iscntrl

int **iscntrl**(int *character*);

Include file: <ctype.h>

Description:

iscntrl returns a nonzero value if the specified character is 127 or is in the range 0 through 31.

character is the ASCII character to be tested.

Example:

```
if (iscntrl(letter))
    printf("Control character\n");
```

Related Functions: isalnum, isalpha, isascii, isdigit, isgraph, islower, isprint, ispunct, isspace, isupper, isxdigit

isdigit

int **isdigit**(int *character*);

Include file: <ctype.h>

Description:

isdigit returns a nonzero value if the specified character is a digit in the range "0" through "9."

character is the ASCII character to be tested.

Example:

```
if (isdigit(letter))
    /* statement */
```

Related Functions: isalnum, isalpha, isascii, iscntrl, isgraph, islower, isprint, ispunct, isspace, isupper, isxdigit

isgraph

int **isgraph**(int *character*);

Include file: <ctype.h>

Description:

isgraph returns a nonzero value if the specified character is a printable character in the range 33 through 126, excluding the space character.

character is the ASCII character to be tested.

Example:

```
if (isgraph(letter))
    putchar(letter);
```

Related Functions: isalnum, isalpha, isascii, iscntrl, isdigit, islower, isprint, ispunct, isspace, isupper, isxdigit

islower

int **islower**(int *character*);

Include file: <ctype.h>

Description:

islower returns a nonzero value if the specified character is a lower-case character in the range "a" through "z."

character is the ASCII character to be tested.

Example:

```
if (islower(letter))
    putchar(toupper(letter));
```

Related Functions: isalnum, isalpha, isascii, iscntrl, isdigit, isgraph, isprint, ispunct, isspace, isupper, isxdigit

isprint

int **isprint**(int *character*);

Include file: <ctype.h>

Description:

isprint returns a nonzero value if the specified character is a printable character in the range 32 through 126.

character is the ASCII character to be tested.

Example:

```
if (isprint(letter))
    putchar(letter);
```

Related Functions: isalnum, isalpha, isascii, iscntrl, isdigit, isgraph, islower, ispunct, isspace, isupper, isxdigit

ispunct

int **ispunct**(int *character*);

Include file: <ctype.h>

Description:

ispunct returns a nonzero value if the specified character is a punctuation character such as a comma, a semicolon, or a period.

character is the ASCII character to be tested.

Example:

```
if (ispunct(letter))
    /* statement */
```

Related Functions: isalnum, isalpha, isascii, iscntrl, isdigit, isgraph, islower, isprint, isspace, isupper, isxdigit

isspace

int **isspace**(int *character*);

Include file: <ctype.h>

Description:

isspace returns a nonzero value if the specified character is a white-space character (tab, linefeed, vertical tab, formfeed, carriage return, or space).

character is the ASCII character to be tested.

Example:

```
while (isspace(letter))
    letter = getchar();
```

Related Functions: isalnum, isalpha, isascii, iscntrl, isdigit, isgraph, islower, isprint, ispunct, isupper, isxdigit

isupper

int **isupper**(char *character*);

Include file: <ctype.h>

Description:

isupper returns a nonzero value if the specified character is an upper-case character in the range "A" through "Z."

character is the ASCII character to be tested.

Example:

```
if (isupper(letter))
    putchar(tolower(letter));
```

Related Functions: isalnum, isalpha, isascii, iscntrl, isdigit, isgraph, islower, isprint, ispunct, isspace, isxdigit

isxdigit

int **isxdigit**(int *character*);

Include file: <ctype.h>

Description:

isxdigit returns a nonzero value if the specified character is a hexadecimal digit in the range "A" through "F," "a" through "f," or "0" through "9."

character is the ASCII character to be tested.

Example:

```
if (isxdigit(letter))
    putchar(letter);
```

Related Functions: isalnum, isalpha, isascii, iscntrl, isdigit, isgraph, islower, isprint, ispunct, isspace, isupper

itoa

char *__itoa__(int *value*, char *__ascii__, int *radix*);

Include file: <stdlib.h>

Description:

itoa converts an integer value to its character-string representation.

value is an integer value to be converted to a character string.

ascii is a character string to which itoa assigns characters.

radix specifies the base value to be used for the conversion. The value 2 is binary, 8 is octal, 10 is decimal, 16 is hexadecimal, and so on.

Example:

```
#include <stdlib.h>

main()
{
    /* display binary, octal, decimal, and hex */
    char buffer[128];
    int i;

    for (i = 0; i < 128; ++i)
        printf("%s %o %d %x\n", itoa(i, buffer, 2),
                i, i, i);
}
```

Related Functions: ltoa, ultoa

j0, j1, jn

See bessel.

kbhit

int __kbhit__(void);

Include file: <conio.h>

Description:

kbhit returns the value 1 if a character is present in the keyboard buffer.

kbhit returns a nonzero value if the user has pressed a key or the value 0 if he or she has not. kbhit does not return the character associated with the key.

Example:

```
#include <conio.h>

main()
{
    while (! kbhit());
}
```

labs

long **labs**(long *expression*);

Include file: <stdlib.h>

Description:

labs returns the absolute value of a long-integer expression.

expression is any long-integer expression.

Example:

```
#include <stdlib.h>

main()
{
    printf("%ld\n", labs(-317412L));
}
```

Related Functions: abs, cabs, fabs

ldexp

double **ldexp**(double *x*, int *exponent*);

Include file: <math.h>

Description:

ldexp returns the value of the specified expression multiplied by the result of 2 raised to the specified exponent.

x is any numeric expression.

exponent is the exponent to which the value 2 is to be raised.

If overflow occurs, ldexp returns the value HUGE_VAL and sets the global variable *errno* to the value ERANGE.

Example:

```
#include <math.h>

main()
{
    printf("%f\n", ldexp(64.0, 10));
}
```

This program produces the following result:

```
65536.000000
```

ldiv

struct ldiv_t **ldiv**(long int *numerator*, long int *denominator*);

Include file: <stdlib.h>

Description:

ldiv returns the quotient and remainder of a long-integer division operation.

ldiv is identical to div except that ldiv works with long-integer values and div works with integer values.

Example: See div.

Related Function: div

lfind

char *__lfind__(char *__key_value__, char *__base__, unsigned *__num_elements__,
        unsigned *__element_size__, int(*__comp__) (void *__a__, void *__b__));

Include file: <search.h>

Description:

lfind searches an array for a specified value.

lfind searches an array in a linear fashion from the first element to the last. lfind supports arrays of all types.

key_value is a pointer to the value for which to search.

base is a pointer to the first element in the array.

num_elements specifies the number of elements in the array.

element_size specifies in bytes the size of each array element.

comp is a pointer to a function that compares two values. If the values are equal, comp returns the value 0. If the values differ, comp returns a nonzero value.

If successful, lfind returns a pointer to the value in the array that matches the key value. If the value is not found, lfind returns the value NULL.

Example:

```
#include <search.h>

main()
{
    static int array[5] = {1, 2, 3, 4, 5};
    int *ptr, comp(int *, int *), value = 4;
    unsigned int num_elements = 5;

    ptr = (int *)lfind((char *)&value, (char *)array,
                       &num_elements, sizeof(int), comp);
    if (*ptr)
        printf("Value %d found at %p\n", *ptr, ptr);
    else
        printf("Value not found\n");
}

comp(int *a, int *b)
{
    return (*a - *b);
}
```

Related Functions: bsearch, lsearch

_lineto

short far **_lineto**(short *x_loc*, short *y_loc*);

Include file: <graph.h>

Description:

_lineto draws a line from the current graphics position to the specified view coordinate using the current line style and color.

x_loc and *y_loc* are the coordinates of the line's end location.

If successful, _lineto returns a nonzero value. If an error occurs, _lineto returns the value 0.

Example:

```
#include <graph.h>
#include <stdio.h>

main()
{
    _setvideomode(_MRES16COLOR);
    _moveto(50, 50);
    _lineto(100, 100);
    getchar();
    _setvideomode(_DEFAULTMODE);
}
```

Related Functions: _moveto, _setlinestyle

localtime

struct tm *__localtime__(time_t *time*);

Include file: <time.h>

Description:

localtime returns a structure that contains the current local time.

The include file time.h defines the structure tm. See gmtime.

time is a pointer to a variable containing the number of seconds since midnight, 01/01/1970. This value is returned by the time function.

Example:

```
#include <time.h>

main()
{
    struct tm *local;
    time_t seconds;
```

(continued)

```
    time(&seconds);
    local = localtime(&seconds);
    printf("%s\n", asctime(local));
}
```

Related Functions: asctime, ctime, ftime, gmtime, time, tzset

locking

int **locking**(int *file_handle*, int *lock_mode*, long *num_bytes*);

Include files: <sys\locking.h> and <io.h>

Description:

locking locks in a file-sharing environment the specified number of bytes starting from the current file position in a file.

file_handle is a file handle associated with a file through the creat or open function.

lock_mode specifies how the file is to be locked. Values and corresponding meanings are as follows:

Value	Meaning
LK_LOCK	if the bytes cannot be locked, waits one second and repeats. After 10 failures, returns an error-status value
LK_NBLCK	if the bytes cannot be locked, returns an error-status value
LK_NBRLCK	same as LK_NBLK
LK_RLCK	same as LK_LOCK
LK_UNLCK	unlocks previously locked bytes

num_bytes is a long-integer value that specifies the number of bytes to lock.

If successful, locking returns the value 0. If an error occurs, locking returns the value −1 and sets the global variable *errno* to one of the following values:

Value	Meaning
EACESS	file already locked
EBADF	file handle invalid
EDEADLOCK	lock operation failed after 10 attempts
EINVAL	invalid parameter

You must install file-sharing support via SHARE.EXE for file-locking to work.

Related Functions: close, creat, open, read, write

---

log

double **log**(double *expression*);

Include file: <math.h>

Description:

log returns the natural logarithm of the specified expression.

expression is any numeric expression.

If the expression is equal to 0, log returns the value –HUGE_VAL and sets the global variable *errno* to the value ERANGE. If the expression is a negative value, log returns the value –HUGE_VAL and sets the global variable *errno* to EDOM.

Example:

```
#include <math.h>

main()
{
    printf("Log of %f is %f\n", 10000.0, log(10000.0));
}
```

Related Functions: exp, log10

---

log10

double **log10**(double *expression*);

Include file: <math.h>

Description:

log10 returns the base 10 logarithm of the specified value.

expression is any numeric expression.

If the expression is equal to 0, log10 returns the value –HUGE_VAL and sets the global variable *errno* to the value ERANGE. If the expression is a negative value, log10 returns the value −HUGE_VAL and sets the global variable *errno* to EDOM.

Example:

```
#include <math.h>

main()
{
    printf("%f %f\n", log10(100), log10(1000));
}
```

Related Functions: exp, log

longjmp

void **longjmp**(jmp_buf *environment*, int *return_value*);

Include file: <setjmp.h>

Description:

longjump performs a nonlocal goto by restoring the stack environment previously saved by the setjmp function.

longjmp works in conjunction with setjmp. The setjmp function sets a location in the program to which control is to be branched, and the longjmp function later branches control to that location.

environment is the environment and location stored by setjmp.

return_value is the value returned when longjmp completes execution.

Example: See setjmp.

Related Function: setjmp

_lrotl

unsigned long **_lrotl**(unsigned long *value*, int *shift_count*);

Include file: <stdlib.h>

Description:

_lrotl rotates an unsigned long-integer value to the left the specified number of bits.

_lrotl shifts the bit in the leftmost position to the rightmost bit position and shifts the remaining bits to the left one position.

value is the unsigned long-integer value to be shifted.

shift_count specifies the number of bit positions by which the value is to be shifted.

Example:

```
#include <stdlib.h>

main()
{
    char buffer[128];
    unsigned long int value = 0xFF;
    int i;

    for (i = 1; i <= 4; i++)
        {
        ltoa(value, buffer, 2);
        printf("%s\n", buffer);
        value = _lrotl(value, i);
        }
}
```

Related Function: _lrotr

_lrotr

unsigned **_lrotr**(unsigned long *value*, int *shift_count*);

Include file: <stdlib.h>

Description:

_lrotr rotates an unsigned long-integer value to the right the specified number of bits.

_lrotr shifts the bit in the rightmost position to the leftmost bit position and shifts the remaining bits to the right one position.

value is the unsigned long-integer value to be shifted.

shift_count specifies the number of bit positions by which the value is to be shifted to the right.

Example: See _lrotl.

Related Function: _lrotl

lsearch

char *lsearch(char *key_value, char *base, unsigned *num_elements,
        unsigned element_size, int(*comp)(void *a, void *b));

Include file: <search.h>

Description:

lsearch searches an array for a specified value. If lsearch does not find
the value, it adds the value to the end of the array.

lsearch searches an array in a linear fashion from the first element to
the last. lsearch supports arrays of all types.

key_value is a pointer to the value for which to search.

base is a pointer to the first element in the array.

num_elements specifies the number of elements in the array.

element_size specifies in bytes the size of each array element.

comp is a pointer to a function that compares two values. If the values
are equal, comp returns the value 0. If the values differ, comp returns
a nonzero value.

If successful, lsearch returns a pointer to the value in the array that
matches the key value. If the value is not found, lsearch returns the
value NULL.

Example: See lfind.

Related Functions: bsearch, lfind

lseek

long lseek(int *file_handle*, long *num_bytes*, int *start_position*);

Include file: <io.h> or <stdlib.h>

Description:

lseek moves the file pointer associated with a file handle the specified
number of bytes starting from the specified offset location.

file_handle is a file handle associated with a file through the creat or
open function.

num_bytes is a long-integer value that specifies the number of bytes
the file pointer is to be moved.

start_position specifies the location from which to begin in the file. Values and corresponding meanings are as follows:

Value	Meaning
SEEK_CUR	seeks from current location
SEEK_END	seeks from end of file
SEEK_SET	seeks from start of file

If successful, lseek returns the new file offset. If an error occurs, lseek returns the value −1 and sets the global variable *errno* to one of the following values:

Value	Meaning
EBADF	file handle invalid
EINVAL	origin or offset invalid

Example:

```
#include <io.h>
#include <fcntl.h>
#include <stdio.h>

main()
{
    int file_handle;
    long position;

    if ((file_handle =
        open("RANDOM.DAT", O_RDONLY)) == -1)
        printf("Error opening RANDOM.DAT\n");
    else
        {
        /* statements */
        position = lseek(file_handle, 100L, SEEK_SET);
        if (position == -1)
            error_handler();
        else
            /* statements */
        }
}
```

Related Functions: creat, open

ltoa

char *ltoa(long int *value*, char *ascii*, int *radix*);

Include file: <stdlib.h>

Description:

ltoa converts a long-integer value to its character-string representation.

value is any long-integer value to be converted into a character string.

ascii is a character string to which ltoa assigns characters.

radix specifies the base value to be used for the conversion. 2 is binary, 8 is octal, 10 is decimal, 16 is hexadecimal, and so on.

Example: See itoa.

Related Functions: itoa, utoa

_makepath

void **_makepath**(char *pathname*, char *drive*, char *directory*,
            char *filename*, char *extension*);

Include file: <stdlib.h>

Description:

_makepath builds a complete pathname from a drive letter, a directory, a filename, and an extension.

_makepath does not create a file or a directory. Instead, _makepath returns the pathname that it builds by using the component parts.

pathname is a character string that will receive the complete pathname.

drive is a character string that contains the desired disk-drive letter.

directory is a character string that contains the desired subdirectory path.

filename is a character string that contains a filename of up to 8 characters.

extension is a character string that contains an extension of up to 3 characters.

Example:

```
#include <stdlib.h>

main()
{
    char pathname[_MAX_PATH];
```

(continued)

```
        _makepath(pathname, "A", "\\SUBDIR\\",
                 "FILENAME", "EXT");
        printf("%s\n", pathname);
}
```

Related Function: _splitpath

malloc, _fmalloc, _nmalloc

void *__malloc__(size_t *num_bytes*);

or

void far *__fmalloc__(size_t *num_bytes*);

or

void near *__nmalloc__(size_t *num_bytes*);

Include file: <malloc.h>

Description:

malloc, _fmalloc, and _nmalloc allocate memory dynamically from the heap.

malloc allocates memory from the default heap; _fmalloc allocates memory from the far heap; _nmalloc allocates memory from the near heap.

num_bytes specifies the number of bytes to be allocated.

If successful, the routines return a pointer to the allocated memory. If an error occurs, they return the value NULL.

Example:

```
#include <malloc.h>
#include <stdio.h>

main()
{
    int *iptr;

    if ((iptr = malloc(1000)) == NULL)
        printf("Error allocating 1000 bytes\n");
    else
        {
        /* statements */
        free(iptr);
        }
}
```

Related Functions: calloc, _ffree, free, _nfree, realloc

matherr

int **matherr**(struct exception *exception_info*);

Include file: <math.h>

Description:

matherr provides a user-defined exception handler for errors in the run-time library math routines.

When the run-time library routines encounter a math exception, they call the matherr routine and pass a pointer to a structure of type exception. By creating this function within your program, you create your own exception handler. The include file math.h defines the structure exception as follows:

```
struct exception
    {
    int type;
    char *name;
    double arg1, arg2;
    double retval;
    };
```

type is an integer value that specifies an error's type. Error types and corresponding meanings are as follows:

Value	Meaning
DOMAIN	domain error
OVERFLOW	overflow in result
PLOSS	loss in significance (partial)
SING	argument singularity
TLOSS	loss in significance (total)
UNDERFLOW	underflow in result

name is a character string that contains the name of the function causing the error.

arg1 and *arg2* are the values causing the error.

retval is the return value from the handler. If the value is 0, C displays an error message and sets the global variable *errno* to an appropriate error value. If the return value is nonzero, C does not display an error message and leaves the global variable *errno* unchanged.

Example:

```
#include <math.h>

main()
{
    double x = -1.0,y;

    y = sqrt(x);
}

int matherr(struct exception *exc)
{
    switch(exc->type)
        {
        case DOMAIN:    printf("DOMAIN error");
                        break;
        case PLOSS:     printf("PLOSS error");
                        break;
        case OVERFLOW:  printf("OVERFLOW error");
                        break;
        case SING:      printf("SING error");
                        break;
        case TLOSS:     printf("TLOSS error");
                        break;
        case UNDERFLOW: printf("UNDERFLOW error");
                        break;
        };
    printf(" in %s; values are %f and %f\n", exc->name,
           exc->arg1, exc->arg2);
    exc->retval = 1;
}
```

This program produces the following result:

```
DOMAIN error in sqrt; values are -1.000000 and 0.000000
```

---

max

max(*x*, *y*);

Include file: <stdlib.h>

Description:

max returns the larger of two values.

max is a macro and therefore works for values of all numeric types.

Example:

```
#include <stdlib.h>

main()
{
    printf("Max is %d\n", max(1, 5));
}
```

Related Function: min

_memavl

size_t **_memavl**(void);

Include file: <malloc.h>

Description:

_memavl returns an unsigned integer that specifies the amount of heap space available for dynamic memory allocation.

Example:

```
#include <malloc.h>
#include <stdio.h>

main()
{
    int *iptr;

    printf("Heap space available: %u\n", _memavl());
    if ((iptr = malloc(1000)) == NULL)
        printf("Error allocating memory\n");
    else
        {
        printf("Heap space available: %u\n", _memavl());
        free(iptr);
        printf("Heap space available: %u\n", _memavl());
        }
}
```

This program produces the following result:

```
Heap space available: 60816
Heap space available: 59812
Heap space available: 60816
```

Related Function: stackavail

memccpy

void *__memccpy__(void *_target_, void *_source_,
                              int _character_, unsigned _num_bytes_);

Include file: <memory.h> or <string.h>

Description:

memccpy copies bytes from one location to another until it either encounters the specified character or has copied the specified number of bytes, whichever occurs first.

target is a pointer to the first byte in the destination buffer.

source is a pointer to the first byte of the bytes to be copied.

character is a character whose first occurrence ends the copy operation.

_num_bytes_ is the maximum number of bytes to be assigned to the target buffer.

If the specified character is copied to the target, memccpy returns a pointer to the position immediately following the character. If the character is not copied, memccpy returns the value NULL.

Example:

```
#include <memory.h>
#include <stdio.h>

main()
{
    char target[128], *pos;

    pos = memccpy(target, "ABCCBA", 'C', 6);
    *pos = NULL;
    printf("%s\n", target);
}
```

This program produces the following result:

ABC

Related Functions: memchr, memcmp, memcpy, memicmp, memmove, memset

memchr

void *__memchr__(const void *_buffer_, int _character_, size_t _num_bytes_);

Include file: <memory.h> or <string.h>

Description:

memchr searches for the first occurrence of the specified character in the first *n* bytes of a memory buffer.

buffer is a pointer to the start of the buffer to be searched for the character.

character is the character for which to search.

num_bytes specifies the maximum number of bytes to be searched for the character.

If memchr locates the character, it returns a pointer to the first occurrence. If memchr does not find the character, it returns the value NULL.

Example:

```
#include <memory.h>

main()
{
    char *pos;

    pos = memchr("Test message", 'm', 12);
    if (*pos)
        /*statements */
    else
        printf("Character not found\n");
}
```

Related Functions: memccpy, memcmp, memcpy, memicmp, memmove, memset

memcmp

int **memcmp**(const void *buffer1*, const void *buffer2*,
              size_t *num_bytes*);

Include file: <memory.h> or <string.h>

Description:

memcmp compares the first *n* bytes of two memory buffers.

buffer1 and *buffer2* are pointers to the starting locations of the buffers to be compared.

num_bytes specifies the number of bytes to be compared.

If the contents of the memory buffers are identical, memcmp returns the value 0. If the first character that differs in *buffer1* is less than the corresponding character in *buffer2*, memchr returns a value less than 0. If the first character that differs in *buffer1* is greater than the corresponding character in *buffer2*, memchr returns a value greater than 0.

Example:

```
#include <memory.h>

main()
{
    printf("ABC and abc: %d\n", memcmp("ABC", "abc", 3));
    printf("ABC and ABC: %d\n", memcmp("ABC", "ABC", 3));
    printf("abc and ABC: %d\n", memcmp("abc", "ABC", 3));
}
```

This program produces the following result:

```
ABC and abc: -1
ABC and ABC: 0
abc and ABC: 1
```

Related Functions: memccpy, memchr, memcpy, memicmp, memmove, memset

memcpy

void *memcpy(void *target, const void *source, size_t num_bytes);

Include file: <memory.h> or <string.h>

Description:

memcpy copies the specified number of bytes from a source buffer to a destination buffer.

target is a pointer to the starting address of the destination buffer.

source is the starting address of the source buffer.

num_bytes specifies the number of bytes to be copied.

Example:

```
#include <memory.h>
```

(continued)

```
main()
{
    struct mycoord
        {
        int x;
        int y;
        } box, savebox;

    box.x = 3;
    box.y = 5;
    memcpy(&savebox, &box, sizeof(struct mycoord));
    printf("%d %d\n", savebox.x, savebox.y);
}
```

Related Functions: memccpy, memchr, memcmp, memicmp, memmove, memset

memicmp

int **memicmp**(void *buffer1*, void *buffer2*, unsigned *num_bytes*);

Include file: <memory.h> or <string.h>

Description:

memicmp compares the first *n* bytes of two memory buffers, ignoring case differences in the letters compared.

memicmp is functionally identical to memcmp except that memicmp does not consider letter case in its comparison.

Example: See memcmp.

Related Functions: memccpy, memchr, memcmp, memcpy, memset, memmove

_memmax

size_t **_memmax**(void);

Include file: <malloc.h> or <stdlib.h>

Description:

_memmax returns the size of the largest contiguous block available for allocation from the near heap.

_memmax is similar to the _memavl function except that _memmax indicates the largest block available from the heap and _memavl indicates the total available heap space.

Example:

```
#include <malloc.h>
#include <stdio.h>

main()
{
    int *ptr;

    if ((ptr = malloc(100)) == NULL)
        printf("Error allocating memory\n");
    else
        {
        printf("_memavl %u _memmax %u\n",
                _memavl(), _memmax());
        free(ptr);
        printf("_memavl %u _memmax %u\n",
                _memavl(), _memmax());
        }
}
```

Related Functions: _memavl, _msize

memmove

void *__memmove__(void *target, const void *source, size_t num_bytes);

Include file: <string.h>

Description:

memmove copies to target memory buffers the specified number of characters from the source.

target is a pointer to the start of the destination buffer.

source is a pointer to the start of the source buffer.

num_bytes specifies the number of characters to be copied.

If the source and target buffers overlap, memmove ensures that the source buffer is copied before being overwritten.

Example:

```
#include <string.h>
```

(continued)

```
main()
{
    char target[128];

    memmove(target, "Source String", 14);
    printf("%s\n", target);
}
```

Related Functions: memccpy, memchr, memcmp, memcpy, memicmp, memset

memset

void ***memset**(void **target*, int *character*, size_t *num_bytes*);

Include file: <memory.h> or <string.h>

Description:

memset sets the first *n* bytes of a memory buffer to the specified value.

target is a pointer to the start of a memory buffer.

character is the value to be assigned to the buffer.

num_bytes specifies the number of bytes that *character* is to be assigned.

Example:

```
#include <memory.h>

main()
{
    char buffer[128];

    memset(buffer, 'A', 128);
    /* statements */
}
```

Related Functions: memccpy, memchr, memcmp, memcpy, memicmp, memmove

min

min(*x*, *y*);

Include file: <stdlib.h>

Description:

min returns the smaller of two values.

min is a macro and works with values of all numeric types.

Example:

```
#include <stdlib.h>

main()
{
    printf("Minimum value is %d\n", min(3, -45));
}
```

Related Function: max

mkdir

int **mkdir**(char *pathname*);

Include file: <direct.h>

Description:

mkdir creates the specified subdirectory.

pathname is a character string that contains the name of the subdirectory to be created.

If successful, mkdir returns the value 0. If an error occurs, mkdir returns the value −1 and sets the global variable *errno* to one of the following values:

Value	Meaning
EACCES	specified name already exists as a file or directory
ENOENT	path not found

Example:

```
#include <direct.h>

main()
{
    if (mkdir("\\TESTDIR") == -1)
        printf("Error creating \\TESTDIR\n");
    else
        printf("\\TESTDIR successfully created\n");
}
```

Related Functions: chdir, rmdir

mktemp

char ***mktemp**(char *template*);

Include file: <io.h>

Description:

mktemp returns a unique filename based on the specified template.

template is a character string that specifies the basic form of the new filename. It consists of two letters, such as PA, followed by six uppercase X's; for example, PAXXXXXX.

mktemp replaces the X's with a combination of alphanumeric characters in order to create a filename that is not currently in use.

If successful, mktemp returns a pointer to the template. If an error occurs, mktemp returns the value NULL.

Example:

```
#include <io.h>
#include <stdio.h>

main()
{
    char *name = "PAXXXXXX";

    if (mktemp(name) == NULL)
        printf("Error creating filename\n");
    else
        printf("Filename created is %s\n", name);
}
```

Related Functions: tempnam, tmpnam

mktime

time_t **mktime**(struct tm *time*);

Include file: <time.h>

Description:

mktime converts a local date to a calendar date.

mktime allows you to determine the calendar date for a date *n* days before or after the current date.

The include file time.h defines the structure tm. See asctime.

If successful, mktime returns the encoded date and time for the calendar date. If an error occurs, mktemp returns the value −1.

Example:

```
#include <time.h>

#define TWO_WEEKS 14

main()
{
    struct tm *future;
    time_t current;

    time(&current);
    future = localtime(&current);
    future->tm_mday += TWO_WEEKS;
    if (mktime(future) == -1)
        printf("Error in mktime\n");
    else
        printf("Two weeks from today is %s\n",
                asctime(future));
}
```

Related Functions: asctime, gmtime, localtime, time

modf

double **modf**(double *expression*, double **intpart*);

Include file: <math.h>

Description:

modf breaks down a floating-point value into its integer and fractional components.

expression is the floating-point expression to be broken down.

intpart is a pointer to a variable of type double to which modf assigns the integer portion of the floating-point expression.

modf returns the fractional part of the expression.

Example:

```
#include <math.h>

main()
{
    double x = 123.4567, intpart, fraction;
```

(continued)

```
    fraction = modf(x, &intpart);
    printf("%f becomes %f and %f\n",
           x, intpart, fraction);
}
```

Related Functions: frexp, ldexp

movedata

void **movedata**(unsigned int *source_segment*,
                unsigned int *source_offset*,
                unsigned int *target_segment*,
                unsigned int *target_offset*,
                unsigned int *num_bytes*);

Include file: <memory.h> or <string.h>

Description:

movedata copies the specified bytes from the location specified by one
segment-and-offset combination to another specified location.

source_segment and *source_offset* combine to create the 32-bit address
of the data to be copied.

target_segment and *target_offset* combine to create the 32-bit address
of the target of the copy operation.

num_bytes specifies the number of bytes to be copied from the source
to the target location.

Example:

```
#include <dos.h>
#include <memory.h>
#include <malloc.h>
#include <stdio.h>

main()
{
    struct emp
        {
        char name[128];
        int age;
        }  far *a, far *b;

    if ((a = _fmalloc(sizeof(struct emp))) == NULL)
        printf("Error allocating memory\n");
    else if ((b = _fmalloc(sizeof(struct emp))) == NULL)
        printf("Error allocating memory\n");
```

(continued)

```
    else
        {
        /* statements */
        movedata(FP_SEG(a), FP_OFF(a), FP_SEG(b),
                FP_OFF(b), sizeof(struct emp));
        /* statements */
        }
}
```

Related Functions: FP_OFF, FP_SEG, memcpy, memmove, segread

_moveto

struct xycoord far **_moveto**(short *xcoord*, short *ycoord*);

Include file: <graph.h>

Description:

_moveto moves the current graphics position to the specified coordinates.

The include file graph.h defines the structure xycoord as follows:

```
struct xycoord
    {
    short xcoord;
    short ycoord;
    };
```

Upon completion, _moveto returns the previous coordinates of the graphics position.

Example: See _lineto.

Related Function: _lineto

_msize, _fmsize, _nmsize

size_t **_msize**(void *ptr*);

or

size_t **_fmsize**(void far *ptr*);

or

size_t **_nmsize**(void near *ptr*);

Include file: <malloc.h>

Description:

_msize, _fmsize, and _nmsize return in bytes the size of a block of dynamically allocated memory.

_msize returns the size of memory allocated from the default heap; _fmsize returns the size of memory allocated from the far heap; and _nmsize returns the size of memory allocated from the near heap.

ptr is a pointer to the start of the memory region.

Example:

```
#include <malloc.h>
#include <stdio.h>

main()
{
    int *ptr;

    if ((ptr = malloc(1000)) == NULL)
        printf("Error allocating memory\n");
    else
        {
        printf("Block size in bytes: %d\n", _msize(ptr));
        free(ptr);
        }
}
```

Related Functions: calloc, malloc, realloc

_nfree

void **_nfree**(void near *buffer*);

Include file: <malloc.h>

Description:

_nfree releases memory previously allocated from the near heap.

buffer is the starting address of a region of memory previously allocated by the _nmalloc function.

Example: See _nmalloc.

Related Functions: _ffree, free, _nmalloc

_nheapchk

See _heapchk.

_nheapset

See _heapset.

_nmalloc

See malloc.

_nmsize

See _msize.

onexit

onexit_t **onexit**(onexit_t *function*);

Include file: <stdlib.h>

Description:

onexit adds a function to the list of functions that C executes when the program completes execution.

onexit is functionally identical to the atexit routine. Because atexit is part of the ANSI standard, you should use it in place of onexit.

Example: See atexit.

Related Functions: atexit, exit

open

int **open**(char *pathname*, int *mode*[, int *create_mode*]);

Include files: <fcntl.h> and <io.h>

Description:

open opens a file as specified and returns a file handle for use in future file input/output operations.

pathname is a character string that specifies the complete pathname of the file to be opened.

mode specifies how the file is to be opened. Values and corresponding meanings are as follows:

Value	Meaning
O_APPEND	opens for append operations
O_BINARY	opens in binary mode
O_CREAT	creates the file if it does not exist
O_EXCL	used with O_CREAT to return an error if the file already exists
O_RDONLY	opens with read-only access
O_RDWR	opens with read/write access
O_TEXT	opens in text mode
O_TRUNC	truncates existing contents
O_WRONLY	opens for write-only access

By using the bitwise OR operator (¦), you can combine two or more modes; for example: O_BINARY ¦ O_RDONLY.

create_mode must be included when you specify O_CREAT. It indicates the file's permission mode. Values and corresponding meanings are as follows:

Value	Meaning
S_IWRITE	write access allowed
S_IREAD	read access allowed
S_IWRITE ¦ S_IREAD	read/write access allowed

If successful, open returns a file handle. If an error occurs, open returns the value −1 and sets the global variable *errno* to one of the following values:

Value	Meaning
EACCES	access violation
EEXIST	file specified with O_CREAT and O_EXCL already exists
EMFILE	too many open files
ENOENT	file not found

Example:

```
#include <fcntl.h>
#include <io.h>

main()
{
    int handle;

    if ((handle =
        open("TEST.DAT", O_RDONLY | O_BINARY)) == -1)
        printf("Error accessing TEST.DAT\n");
    else
        {
        /* statements */
        close(handle);
        }
}
```

Related Functions: close, creat, fopen

outp

int **outp**(unsigned *port_address*, int *value*);

Include file: <conio.h>

Description:

outp outputs a byte value to the specified port address.

port_address is an unsigned integer from 0 through 65,535 that specifies the address of the desired port.

value is the byte value to be output to the port.

outp returns the value that it outputs to the port.

Example: See inp.

Related Functions: inp, outpw

outpw

int **outpw**(unsigned *port_address*, unsigned *value*);

Include file: <conio.h>

Description:

outpw outputs a 16-bit value to the specified port address.

port_address is an unsigned integer from 0 through 65,535 that specifies the address of the desired port.

value is the integer value to be output to the port.

outpw returns the value that it writes to the port.

Example: See inp.

Related Functions: inp, outp

_outtext

void far **_outtext**(char far *text*);

Include file: <graph.h>

Description:

_outtext writes text to the current video page and text window.

_outtext allows you to write text in the current text color and in the current text window.

text is a character string that contains the text to be written.

Example:

```
#include <graph.h>

main()
{
    int color;
    char text[128];

    for (color = 0; color < 32; color++)
        {
        sprintf(text, "Current color is %d\n", color);
```

(continued)

```
        _settextcolor(color);
        _outtext(text);
        }
}
```

Related Functions: _settextcolor, _settextposition, _settextwindow, _wrapon

perror

void **perror**(const char *message);

Include file: <stdio.h>

Description:

perror sends to stderr a program-defined error message that is followed by the system error message for the last library call that failed.

message is a character string that contains the program-defined error message.

perror obtains the error message for the system error from the array sys_errlist.

perror uses the global variable *errno* as an index to the corresponding error message.

Example:

```
#include <fcntl.h>
#include <stdio.h>

main()
{
    int file_handle;

    if ((file_handle = open("TEST.DAT", O_RDONLY)) == -1)
        perror("Error opening TEST.DAT");
    else
        /* statements */
}
```

Related Functions: clearerr, ferror, strerror

_pie

short far **_pie**(short *fill_flag*, short *xleft*, short *ytop*,
                short *xright*, short *ybottom*,
                short *xstart*, short *ystart*,
                short *xstop*, short *ystop*);

Include file: <graph.h>

Description:

_pie draws a pie-shaped wedge in graphics mode.

_pie draws a wedge shape inside a rectangle bounded by the coordinates (*xleft*, *ytop*) and (*xright*, *ybottom*).

The pie's arc begins at the coordinate that intersects the vector at (*xstart*, *ystart*). The arc ends at the coordinate that intersects (*xstop*, *ystop*).

fill_flag specifies whether the pie is to be filled with the current color and fill pattern. Values and corresponding meanings are as follows:

Value	*Meaning*
_GBORDER	do not fill
_GFILLINTERIOR	fill the pie shape

Example:

```
#include <graph.h>
#include <stdio.h>

main()
{
    _setvideomode(_MRES16COLOR);
    _pie(_GBORDER, 10, 10, 80, 80, 20, 20, 60, 120);
    getchar();
    _setvideomode(_DEFAULTMODE);
}
```

Related Functions: _arc, _ellipse, _rectangle

pow

double **pow**(double *expression*, double *power*);

Include file: <math.h>

Description:

pow returns the resulting value of a specified value raised to a specified power.

expression is any numeric expression.

power specifies the power to which the expression is to be raised.

If the expression is equal to 0 and the specified power is a negative value, pow returns the value HUGE_VAL and sets the global variable *errno* to the value EDOM. Likewise, if the expression is negative and the power is not an integer, pow returns HUGE_VAL and sets *errno* to EDOM. If overflow occurs, pow returns HUGE_VAL and sets *errno* to ERANGE.

Example:

```
#include <math.h>

main()
{
    int i;

    for (i = 0; i < 5; i++)
        printf("10 raised to %d is %f\n", i,
                pow(10.0, i));
}
```

This program produces the following result:

```
10 raised to 0 is 1.000000
10 raised to 1 is 10.000000
10 raised to 2 is 100.000000
10 raised to 3 is 1000.000000
10 raised to 4 is 10000.000000
```

Related Functions: exp, log, sqrt

---

printf

int **printf**(const char *format_specification[, argument]...);

Include file: <stdio.h>

Description:

printf sends formatted output to stdout.

format_specification is a character string that specifies how output is displayed on screen. It can contain format specifications that direct printf to display values in a variety of forms, including decimal, octal, hexadecimal, and floating-point. The following are valid format specifiers:

Code	Meaning
%d	decimal integer
%i	decimal integer
%u	unsigned decimal integer
%o	unsigned octal integer
%x	unsigned hexadecimal integer using lowercase letters a through f
%X	unsigned hexadecimal integer using uppercase letters A through F
%f	double-precision value
%e	double-precision value in exponential format
%E	double-precision value in exponential format using an uppercase E
%g	double-precision value. If the exponent is less than −4 or greater than the precision argument, exponential format is used; otherwise, standard floating-point format is used
%G	same as %g except that an uppercase E is used for exponential format
%c	single ASCII character
%s	null-terminated character string
%n	assigns the number of characters printed thus far to a variable of type int
%p	far pointer value

printf also allows you to precede each format specifier with a plus (+) or minus (−) sign. A plus sign directs printf to display the value's sign. A minus sign directs printf to left-justify the field.

printf also supports width and precision specifiers in the form *width.precision. width* specifies the number of characters in the output field. *precision* specifies either the number of digits to the right of the decimal point or the total number of significant digits.

Example:

```
#include <stdio.h>

main()
{
    float x = 123.456789;
    int i = 100;
```

(continued)

```
    printf("%+d %05d %x\n", i, i, i);
    printf("%f %6.3f %10.5f\n", x, x, x);
}
```

This program produces the following result:

```
+100 00100 64
123.456787 123.457   123.45679
```

Related Functions: fprintf, sprintf, vprintf

putc

int **putc**(int *character*, FILE **file_pointer*);

Include file: <stdio.h>

Description:

putc writes a specified character to a specified file.

character is the ASCII character to be written to the file.

file_pointer is a file pointer associated with a file through the fdopen, fopen, or freopen function.

If successful, putc returns the character written. If an error occurs, putc returns the value EOF.

Example:

```
#include <stdio.h>

main(int argc, char *argv[])
{
    /* copy the contents of one file to another */
    FILE *input, *output;
    int letter;

    if (argc < 3)
        printf("Must specify source and target files\n");
    else
        {
        if ((input = fopen(argv[1], "r")) == NULL)
            printf("Error opening %s\n", argv[1]);
        else if ((output = fopen(argv[2], "w")) == NULL)
            printf("Error opening %s\n", argv[2]);
        else
            {
            while (! feof(input))
                {
```

(continued)

```
                letter = getc(input);
                putc(letter, output);
                }
            fclose(input);
            fclose(output);
            }
        }
}
```

Related Functions: fputc, getc, putchar

putch

int **putch**(int *letter*);

Include file: <conio.h>

Description:

putch writes a specified character directly to the console.

letter is the character to be written to the console.

If successful, putch returns the letter written. If an error occurs, putch returns the value EOF.

Example:

```
#include <conio.h>

main()
{
    int letter;

    for (letter = 'A'; letter <= 'Z'; letter++)
        putch(letter);
}
```

Related Functions: fputc, getch, putc, putchar

putchar

int **putchar**(int *letter*);

Include file: <stdio.h>

Description:

putchar sends a specified character to stdout.

letter is the character to be written to stdout.

If successful, putchar returns the character written. If an error occurs, putchar returns the value EOF.

Example:

```
#include <stdio.h>

main(int argc, char *argv[])
{
    /* Display a file's contents */
    int letter;
    FILE *fp;

    if ((fp = fopen(argv[1], "r")) == NULL)
        printf("Error accessing %s\n", argv[1]);
    else
        {
        while (! feof(fp))
            {
            letter = getc(fp);
            putchar(letter);
            }
        fclose(fp);
        }
}
```

Related Functions: fputchar, getchar, putc

putenv

int **putenv**(char *environment_entry*);

Include file: <stdlib.h>

Description:

putenv adds or changes an entry in the DOS environment table.

putenv adds an entry to the process environment table. When the program completes execution, the entry no longer exists.

environment_entry is a character string in the format *variable=value* that specifies the desired environment entry.

If successful, putenv returns the value 0. If an error occurs, putenv returns the value −1.

Example:

```
#include <stdlib.h>

main()
{
    if (putenv("TEST=Test environment entry") == -1)
        printf("Error adding TEST entry\n");
    else
        printf("TEST entry set to %s\n", getenv("TEST"));
}
```

Related Function: getenv

_putimage

void far **_putimage**(short *x_loc*, short *y_loc*,
                        char far *image_buffer*, short *display_flag*);

Include file: <graph.h>

Description:

_putimage writes to the screen a graphics image previously saved to a buffer by the _getimage function.

x_loc and *y_loc* specify the coordinates of the upper-left corner of the image.

image_buffer is a memory buffer that contains the graphics image previously saved by the _getimage function.

display_flag specifies how _putimage displays the graphics image on the screen. Values and corresponding meanings are as follows:

Value	Meaning
_GAND	performs a logical AND of the graphics image and the image that currently exists in that location
_GOR	performs a logical OR of the graphics image and the image that currently exists in that location
_GPRESET	places the image on the screen, inverting the pixels of the image as saved by the _getimage function
_GPSET	places the image on the screen in the form in which it was saved by the _getimage function
_GXOR	performs an exclusive OR of the graphics image and the image that currently exists in that location

Example:

```
#include <graph.h>
#include <stdio.h>
#include <stdlib.h>

main()
{
    char *buffer;
    int oldrow, oldcolumn, row, column;

    buffer = malloc(_imagesize(0, 0, 10, 10));
    _setvideomode(_MRES16COLOR);
    _rectangle(_GFILLINTERIOR, 0, 0, 10, 10);
    _getimage(0, 0, 10, 10, buffer);
    oldrow = 0;
    oldcolumn = 0;
    while (! kbhit())
        {
        _putimage(oldrow, oldcolumn, buffer,
                  _GXOR); /* erase old */
        _putimage(row, column, buffer, _GXOR);
        oldrow = row;
        oldcolumn = column;
        row = (rand() / 32767.0) * 320;
        column = (rand() / 32767.0) * 200;
        }
    _setvideomode(_DEFAULTMODE);
}
```

Related Function: _getimage

puts

int **puts**(const char *string*);

Include file: <stdio.h>

Description:

puts writes a null-terminated character string to stdout. When puts encounters the NULL character, it writes a newline character (\n).

string is the character string to be written to stdout. If successful, puts returns the value 0. If an error occurs, puts returns a nonzero value.

Example:

```
#include <stdio.h>
```

(continued)

```
main()
{
    puts("Test message");
}
```

Related Functions: gets, putc

putw

int **putw**(int *value*, FILE **file_pointer*);

Include file: <stdio.h>

Description:

putw writes an integer value to a specified file.

value is an integer value to be written to a file.

file_pointer is a file pointer associated with a file through the fdopen, fopen, or freopen function.

If successful, putw returns the integer value it writes to the specified file. If an error occurs, putw returns the value EOF.

Example: See getw.

Related Function: getw

qsort

void **qsort**(void **base_address*,
            size_t *num_elements*, size_t *element_width*,
            int (**comp*)(const void **a*, const void **b*));

Include file: <stdlib.h> or <search.h>

Description:

qsort sorts an array of values using a quick-sort algorithm.

base_address is a pointer to the starting address of the array to be sorted.

num_elements specifies the number of elements in the array.

element_width specifies in bytes the size of each array element.

comp is a pointer to a program-defined function that compares two values referenced by pointers. If the first value is larger than the second, comp returns a value greater than 0. If the first value is the same as the second, comp returns the value 0. If the first value is less than the second, comp returns a value less than 0.

Example:

```
#include <search.h>

main()
{
    static int a[10] = {10, 1, 9, 8, 2, 7, 4, 6, 5, 3};
    int i;
    int comp(int *, int *);

    qsort(a, 10, sizeof(int), comp);

    for (i = 0; i < 10; ++i)
        printf("%d\n", a[i]);
}

int comp(int *a, int *b)
{
    return(*a - *b);
}
```

Related Functions: bsearch, lfind, lsearch

raise

int **raise**(int *signal*);

Include file: <signal.h>

Description:

raise raises a signal to test exception-handling routines installed by the signal function.

signal is an integer value that specifies the signal to be raised. The value must be one of the following:

Value	Usage
SIGABRT	program termination with an exit status of 3
SIGFPE	floating-point error
SIGILL	illegal instruction

(continued)

Value	Usage
SIGINT	interrupt 0x23 (Ctrl+C)
SIGSEGV	illegal storage access
SIGTERM	termination request

Unless you have installed an exception handler for a specific signal, the default action for that signal is performed.

Example:

```
#include <signal.h>

main()
{
    void signal_handler(void);

    if (signal(SIGINT, signal_handler) == SIG_ERR)
        printf("Error installing handler\n");
    else
        raise(SIGINT);
}

void signal_handler(void)
{
    printf("In handler\n");
}
```

Related Function: signal

rand

int **rand**(void);

Include file: <stdlib.h>

Description:

rand returns a pseudorandom number in the range 0 through 32,767.

To set the random-number generator's initial seed, use the srand function.

Example:

```
#include <stdlib.h>
```

(continued)

```
main()
{
    int i;

    for (i = 0; i < 10; ++i)
        printf("%d %d\n", i, rand());
}
```

Related Function: srand

read

int **read**(int *file_handle*, char **buffer*, unsigned int *num_bytes*);

Include file: <io.h>

Description:

read reads into a buffer data from a file associated with a specified file handle.

file_handle is a handle associated with a file through the open function.

buffer is a data buffer used for input.

num_bytes specifies the number of bytes to be read from the desired file.

If successful, read returns a count of the number of bytes read into the buffer. If an error occurs, read returns the value −1 and sets the global variable *errno* to the value EBADF.

Example:

```
#include <stdio.h>
#include <fcntl.h>
#include <io.h>

/* display a file's contents */

main(int argc, char *argv[])
{
    char buffer[128];
    int file_handle, bytes_read;

    if ((file_handle = open(argv[1], O_RDONLY)) == -1)
        printf("Error opening %s\n", argv[1]);
    else
        {
        while (! eof(file_handle))
            {
```

(continued)

```
            bytes_read = read(file_handle, buffer,
                              sizeof(buffer));
            buffer[bytes_read] = NULL;
            puts(buffer);
            }
        close(file_handle);
        }
}
```

Related Functions: creat, fread, open, write

realloc

void *__realloc__(void *ptr, size_t desired_size);

Include file: <malloc.h> or <stdlib.h>

Description:

realloc changes the size of a previously allocated block of memory.

ptr is a pointer to a block of memory previously allocated by the calloc or malloc function.

desired_size specifies the desired number of bytes for the reallocation.

If successful, realloc returns a pointer to the new memory region. If realloc is unable to allocate the specified amount of memory, it returns the value NULL.

Example:

```
#include <malloc.h>
#include <stdio.h>

main()
{
    char *ptr;

    if ((ptr = malloc(200)) == NULL)
        printf("Unable to initially allocate memory\n");
    else if ((ptr = realloc(ptr, 1000)) == NULL)
        printf("Unable to reallocate memory\n");
    else
        printf("Allocation adjusted to 1000 bytes\n");
}
```

Related Functions: calloc, free, malloc

_rectangle

short far **_rectangle**(short *fill_flag*, short *x_left*, short *y_top*,
short *x_right*, short *y_bottom*);

Include file: <graph.h>

Description:

_rectangle draws a rectangle on the screen using the specified
coordinates.

fill_flag specifies whether _rectangle fills the rectangle with the current color and fill pattern. Values and corresponding meanings are as
follows:

Value	Meaning
_GBORDER	do not fill rectangle
_GFILLINTERIOR	fill rectangle

The coordinates (*x_left*, *y_top*) and (*x_right*, *y_bottom*) specify op-
posite corners of the rectangle.

If successful, _rectangle returns a nonzero value. If an error occurs,
_rectangle returns the value 0.

Example:

```
#include <graph.h>
#include <stdio.h>

main()
{
    _setvideomode(_MRES16COLOR);
    _rectangle(_GBORDER, 50, 50, 150, 150);
    _rectangle(_GFILLINTERIOR, 160, 50, 300, 150);
    getchar();
    _setvideomode(_DEFAULTMODE);
}
```

Related Functions: _setcolor, _setlinestyle, _setvideomode

_remapallpalette

short far **_remapallpalette**(long far *colors*);

Include file: <graph.h>

Description:

_remapallpalette changes the graphics palette colors.

The current video mode determines the number of colors supported for graphics. The default colors are as follows:

Value	Color	Value	Color
0	black	8	dark gray
1	blue	9	light blue
2	green	10	light green
3	cyan	11	light cyan
4	red	12	light red
5	magenta	13	light magenta
6	brown	14	yellow
7	white	15	bright white

In four-color mode, for example, only the colors 0 through 3 are supported. The _remapallpalette routine allows you to assign the desired colors to the current palette.

colors is an array of long-integer values that contains the colors to map to the current palette.

If successful, _remapallpalette returns the value 0. If an error occurs, it returns the value −1.

Example:

```
#include <graph.h>
#include <stdio.h>

main()
{
    static long colors[16] = {_RED, _WHITE, _BLUE,
            _GREEN, _GRAY, _CYAN, _MAGENTA, _BROWN,
            _LIGHTBLUE, _LIGHTGREEN, _BRIGHTWHITE,
            _LIGHTYELLOW, _LIGHTCYAN, _LIGHTRED,
            _LIGHTMAGENTA, _BLACK};
    int color;

    _setvideomode(_MRES16COLOR);
    for (color = 0; color < 16; color++)
        {
        _setcolor(color);
        _rectangle(_GFILLINTERIOR, color * 10, 0,
                (color + 1) * 10, 20);
        }
    getchar();
    _remapallpalette(colors);
    getchar();
    _setvideomode(_DEFAULTMODE);
}
```

_remappalette

long far **_remappalette**(short *pixelcolor*, long *color*);

Include file: <graph.h>

Description:

_remappalette reassigns a color value in the current palette.

pixelcolor is the current palette color to be reassigned.

color is a long-integer value that specifies the desired color.

If successful, _remappalette returns the previous palette color. If an error occurs, it returns the value −1.

Example:

```
#include <graph.h>
#include <stdio.h>

main()
{
    int color;

    _setvideomode(_MRES4COLOR);
    for (color = 0; color < 4; color++)
        {
        _setcolor(color);
        _rectangle(_GFILLINTERIOR, color * 10, 10,
                    (color + 1) * 10, 30);
        }
    getchar();
    _remappalette(0, _RED);
    getchar();
    _setvideomode(_DEFAULTMODE);
}
```

Related Functions: _remapallpalette, _setcolor

remove

int **remove**(const char *pathname*);

Include file: <io.h> or <stdio.h>

Description:

remove deletes a specified file from disk.

pathname is a character string that contains the complete pathname of the file to be deleted.

If successful, remove returns the value 0. If an error occurs, remove returns the value −1 and sets the global variable *errno* to one of the following values:

Value	Meaning
EACCES	read-only file
ENOENT	file not found

Example:

```
#include <stdio.h>

main(int argc, char *argv[])
{
    if (remove(argv[1]) == -1)
        printf("Error deleting %s\n", argv[1]);
    else
        printf("%s deleted\n", argv[1]);
}
```

Related Function: unlink

rename

int **rename**(const char ∗*oldname*, const char ∗*newname*);

Include file: <io.h> or <stdio.h>

Description:

rename renames an existing file.

oldname is a character string that contains the pathname of the file to be renamed.

newname is a character string that contains the desired pathname for the file.

rename allows you to move a file from one subdirectory to another but not from one device to another.

If successful, rename returns the value 0. If an error occurs, rename returns a nonzero value and sets the global variable *errno* to one of the following values:

Value	Meaning
EACCES	access denied—target file might already exist
ENOENT	file not found
EXDEV	cannot move a file from one device to another

Example:

```c
#include <stdio.h>

main(int argc, char *argv[])
{
    if (argc < 3)
        printf("Specify oldname and newname\n");
    else if (rename(argv[1], argv[2]) != 0)
        printf("Error renaming file\n");
    else
        printf("File successfully renamed\n");
}
```

rewind

void **rewind**(FILE *file_pointer);

Include file: <stdio.h>

Description:

rewind resets a file pointer to the beginning of a file.

file_pointer is a file pointer associated with a file through the fdopen, fopen, or freopen function.

Example:

```c
#include <stdio.h>

main()
{
    FILE *fp;
    int lines = 0;
    char buffer[128];

    if ((fp = fopen("TEST.DAT", "r")) == NULL)
        printf("Error accessing TEST.DAT\n");
    else
        {
        /* count the number of lines in the file */
        while (fgets(buffer, sizeof(buffer), fp))
            lines ++;
```

(continued)

```
                    /* rewind and start processing */
                    rewind(fp);
                    /* statements */
                    }
}
```

Related Function: fseek

rmdir

int **rmdir**(char *pathname*);

Include file: <direct.h>

Description:

rmdir removes a specified directory.

pathname is a character string that contains the name of the subdirectory to be deleted.

If successful, rmdir returns the value 0. If an error occurs, rmdir returns the value −1 and sets the global variable *errno* to one of the following values:

Value	*Meaning*
EACCES	access denied—cannot delete the current directory or a directory containing files
ENOENT	directory not found

Example:

```
#include <direct.h>

main(int argc, char *argv[])
{
    if (rmdir(argv[1]) == -1)
        printf("Error deleting directory\n");
    else
        printf("%s successfully removed\n", argv[1]);
}
```

Related Functions: chdir, mkdir

rmtmp

int **rmtmp**(void);

Include file: <stdio.h>

Description:

rmtmp removes from the current directory all files created by the tmpfile function.

Upon completion, rmtmp returns the number of files that it closed and deleted successfully.

Example: See tmpfile.

Related Functions: flushall, tmpfile

_rotl

unsigned int **_rotl**(unsigned int *value*, int *num_shifts*);

Include file: <stdlib.h>

Description:

_rotl rotates the bits of an unsigned integer to the left the specified number of bits.

_rotl shifts bits in a circular fashion. The leftmost bit becomes the rightmost (least significant) bit, and the remaining bits are moved to the left one position.

value is the unsigned integer value to be shifted left.

num_shifts specifies the number of shift operations to be performed.

Example:

```
#include <stdlib.h>

main()
{
    unsigned int value = 1;
    int count;

    for (count = 1; count < 16; count++)
        printf("%x\n", _rotl(value, count));
}
```

Related Functions: _lrotl, _lrotr, _rotr

_rotr

unsigned int **_rotr**(unsigned int *value*, int *num_shifts*);

Include file: <stdlib.h>

Description:

_rotr rotates the bits of an unsigned integer to the right the specified number of bits.

_rotr shifts bits in a circular fashion. The rightmost bit becomes the leftmost (most significant) bit, and the remaining bits are moved to the right one position.

value is the unsigned integer value to be shifted right.

num_shifts specifies the number of shift operations to be performed.

Example:

```
#include <stdlib.h>

main()
{
    unsigned int value = 4;
    int count;

    for (count = 1; count < 16; count++)
        printf("%x\n", _rotr(value, count));
}
```

Related Functions: _lrotl, _lrotr, _rotl

sbrk

void *sbrk(int *increment*);

Include file: <malloc.h>

Description:

sbrk changes the location of a program's break value (the address of the first value beyond the heap).

increment is the number of bytes to add to or subtract from the break address.

If successful, sbrk returns the previous break address. If an error occurs, sbrk returns the value −1 and sets the global variable *errno* to the value ENOMEM.

Example:

```
#include <malloc.h>

main()
{
    printf("Current break value is %p\n", sbrk(0));
}
```

Related Functions: calloc, free, malloc, realloc

scanf

int **scanf**(const char *format_specifications[, argument]...);

Include file: <stdio.h>

Description:

scanf reads data from stdin into the specified variables.

format_specifications is a character string that contains the format specifications for the input data. The format specifications are preceded by a percent sign (%).

Value type	Meaning
%d	value of type int
%i	value of type int
%D	value of type long
%I	value of type long
%o	octal value of type int
%O	octal value of type long
%x	hexadecimal value of type int
%X	hexadecimal value of type long
%u	value of type unsigned int
%U	value of type unsigned long
%e, %E	value of type float in exponential format
%f	value of type float
%g, %G	value of type float in standard or exponential format
%c	value of type char
%s	character-string value
%n	number of characters read so far
%p	far pointer value

Each argument must be a pointer to a variable to which scanf assigns values.

To read strings that are not delimited by space characters, you can substitute a set of characters in brackets ([ ]) for the string type character(s). The corresponding input field is read up to the first character that does not appear in the bracketed character set.

If the first character in the brackets is a caret (^), the effect is reversed: scanf terminates the string input on the first character that appears in the bracketed set of characters.

Upon completion, scanf returns the number of variables to which it successfully assigned values. If end-of-file occurs, scanf returns the value EOF.

Example:

```
#include <stdio.h>

main()
{
    int a;
    float b;

    printf("Enter an integer followed by a float\n");
    scanf("%d %f", &a, &b);
    printf("Values entered: %d %f\n", a, b);
}
```

Related Functions: cscanf, fscanf

_searchenv

void **_searchenv**(char *filename*, char *environment_entry*,
                    char *pathname*);

Include file: <stdlib.h>

Description:

_searchenv searches the directory path associated with a specified environment entry for a specified file.

The DOS environment can contain entries for directory paths such as PATH, APPEND, LIB, and INCLUDE. _searchenv allows you to search the directories associated with one of these entries for a file.

filename is a character string that contains the filename for which to search.

environment_entry is a character string that contains the environment variable, such as PATH or LIB, to be examined.

pathname is a character string buffer to which _searchenv assigns the complete pathname of the specified file if it successfully locates the file. If _searchenv fails to locate the file, *pathname* will contain an empty null-terminated string.

Example:

```
#include <stdlib.h>

main()
{
    char pathname[_MAX_PATH];

    _searchenv("DISKCOPY.COM", "PATH", pathname);
    if (*pathname)
        printf("Complete pathname is %s\n", pathname);
    else
        printf("DISKCOPY.COM not found in PATH\n");
}
```

Related Functions: getenv, putenv

segread

void **segread**(struct SREGS *segment_registers*);

Include file: <dos.h>

Description:

segread places the current values of the segment registers ES, CS, SS, and DS into a structure of type SREGS.

segment_registers is a pointer to a structure of type SREGS defined in the include file dos.h as follows:

```
struct SREGS
    {
    unsigned int es;
    unsigned int cs;
    unsigned int ss;
    unsigned int ds;
    };
```

Several of the BIOS and DOS services require you to supply segment register values.

Example:

```
#include <dos.h>

main()
{
    struct SREGS segment_registers;

    segread(&segment_registers);
    printf("CS %x; DS %x; ES %x; SS %x\n",
            segment_registers.cs, segment_registers.ds,
            segment_registers.es, segment_registers.ss);
}
```

Related Functions: int86x, intdosx

_selectpalette

short far **_selectpalette**(short *palette_number*);

Include file: <graph.h>

Description:

_selectpalette selects a background and a set of three colors for use in _MRES4COLOR and _MRESNOCOLOR graphics modes.

In _MRES4COLOR mode, _selectpalette lets you select one of the four predefined palettes shown below:

Palette number	*Colors*
0	green, red, brown
1	cyan, magenta, light gray
2	light green, light red, yellow
3	light cyan, light magenta, white

In _MRESNOCOLOR mode on a CGA system, _selectpalette lets you select one of the two predefined palettes shown below:

Palette number	*Colors*
0	blue, red, light gray
1	light blue, light red, white

In _MRESNOCOLOR mode on an EGA system, _selectpalette lets you select one of the following three predefined palettes:

Palette number	Colors
0	green, red, brown
1	light green, light red, yellow
2	light cyan, light red, yellow

Example:

```
#include <graph.h>
#include <stdio.h>

main()
{
    int color, palette;

    _setvideomode(_MRES4COLOR);
    for (color = 1; color < 4; color++)
        {
        _setcolor(color);
        _rectangle(_GFILLINTERIOR, 20 * color, 0,
                   20 * (color + 1), 20);
        }
    for (palette = 0; palette < 4; palette++)
        {
        _selectpalette(palette);
        getchar();
        }
    _setvideomode(_DEFAULTMODE);
}
```

Related Functions: _setcolor, _setvideomode

_setactivepage

short far **_setactivepage**(short *video_page*);

Include file: <graph.h>

Description:

_setactivepage selects the video-display page to which graphics output or output from _outtext is to be written.

The active page is the video-display page to which graphics output is to be written. The visual page is the video-display page that is visible on your screen.

The available number of video-display pages is dependent upon your adapter type. See _getvideoconfig.

Your output will appear instantaneously if you first write it to a video-display page and then make the page visible.

If successful, _setactivepage returns the page number of the previous active page. If an error occurs, it returns a negative value.

Example:

```
#include <stdio.h>
#include <graph.h>

main()
{
    int save_page, row;

    if (_setactivepage(1) < 0)
        printf("Error changing active page\n");
    else
        {
        for (row = 0; row < 25; row++)
            {
            _settextposition(row, 0);
            _outtext("Page 1 output");
            }
        save_page = _setvisualpage(1);   /* show output */
        getchar();
        _setvisualpage(save_page);
        }
}
```

Related Functions: _getvideoconfig, _setvisualpage

_setbkcolor

long far **_setbkcolor**(long *color*);

Include file: <graph.h>

Description:

_setbkcolor sets the current background color to the specified pixel color value.

color is a long-integer value that specifies the desired background color.

Upon completion, _setbkcolor returns the pixel color value of the previous background color.

Example:

```
#include <stdio.h>
#include <graph.h>

main()
{
    long int color;
    char buffer[128];

    for (color = 0; color < 16; color++)
        {
        _setbkcolor(color);
        _clearscreen(_GCLEARSCREEN);
        sprintf(buffer, "Current color %d\n", color);
        _outtext(buffer);
        getchar();
        }
    _setvideomode(_DEFAULTMODE);
}
```

Related Function: _getbkcolor

setbuf

void **setbuf**(FILE *file_pointer, char *buffer);

Include file: <stdio.h>

Description:

setbuf specifies the buffer used for disk input/output operations.

file_pointer is a newly opened file pointer that has not been used for read or write operations.

buffer is a pointer to a buffer of at least BUFSIZ bytes as defined in the include file stdio.h.

Example:

```
#include <stdio.h>

main()
{
    char buffer[BUFSIZ];
    FILE *fp;

    if ((fp = fopen("TEST.DAT", "r")) == NULL)
        printf("Error opening TEST.DAT\n");
    else
```

(continued)

```
        {
        setbuf(fp, buffer);
        /* statements */
        }
}
```

Related Functions: fclose, fflush

_setcliprgn

void far **_setcliprgn**(short *x_left*, short *y_top*,
                        short *x_right*, short *y_bottom*);

Include file: <graph.h>

Description:

_setcliprgn defines the coordinates of the graphics clipping region.

A clipping region defines an area on the screen to which graphics output can be displayed. Graphics output that exceeds this region is "clipped" and does not appear on screen.

The coordinates (*x_left*, *y_top*) and (*x_right*, *y_bottom*) specify the upper-left and lower-right corners of the rectangle that defines the clipping region.

Example:

```
#include <graph.h>
#include <stdio.h>

main()
{
    _setvideomode(_MRES16COLOR);
    _setcliprgn(0, 0, 75, 75);
    _ellipse(_GFILLINTERIOR, 30, 30, 100, 100);
    getchar();
    _setvideomode(_DEFAULTMODE);
}
```

Related Functions: _settextwindow, _setvieworg, _setviewport

_setcolor

short far **_setcolor**(short *color*);

Include file: <graph.h>

Description:

_setcolor sets the current graphics foreground color.

_setcolor works only in graphics mode. To set the color for text output displayed by _outtext, use the _settextcolor function.

Example: See _remapallpalette.

Related Functions: _getcolor, _selectpalette

_setfillmask

void **_setfillmask**(unsigned char far *fill_mask*);

Include file: <graph.h>

Description:

_setfillmask defines the fill mask used for graphics operations.

fill_mask is a pointer to an array of characters that represent the bits of an 8×8 array. If a bit is set (1), the pixel that corresponds to that position is turned on. If the bit is clear (0), the pixel is left off. By changing the bit values, you can change the patterns used in fill operations.

Example:

```
#include <graph.h>
#include <stdio.h>

main()
{
    static char mask[8] = {0, 0xFF, 0, 0xFF,
                           0, 0xFF, 0, 0xFF};

    _setvideomode(_MRES16COLOR);
    _setfillmask(mask);
    _rectangle(_GFILLINTERIOR, 0, 0, 100, 100);
    getchar();
    _setvideomode(_DEFAULTMODE);
}
```

Related Functions: _floodfill, _getfillmask

setjmp

int **setjmp**(jmp_buf *environment*);

Include file: <setjmp.h>

Description:

setjmp saves the current stack for later use by the longjmp function.
Used together, setjmp and longjmp provide a way to perform nonlocal
branching.

The include file setjmp.h defines the variable type jmp_buf. When
setjmp saves the stack environment, it returns the value 0. When
setjmp returns as a result of a call to longjmp, setjmp returns the value
specified as an argument to longjmp, or, if the value argument of
longjmp is 0, it returns the value 1.

Example:

```
#include <setjmp.h>

jmp_buf state;    /* global variable */

main()
{
    void some_function(void);

    if (setjmp(state) == 0)
        printf("Saved setjmp state\n");
    else
        {
        printf("Return from longjmp\n");
        exit(0);
        }
    some_function();
}

void some_function(void)
{
    printf("In some_function\n");
    longjmp(state, -1);
}
```

Related Function: longjmp

_setlinestyle

void far **_setlinestyle**(unsigned short *line_style*);

Include file: <graph.h>

Description:

_setlinestyle selects the mask used for line drawing.

The mask is a 16-bit value in which each bit represents a pixel in the line being drawn. If a bit is set (1), the corresponding pixel is changed to the current color. If a bit is clear (0), the corresponding pixel is left unchanged. The template is repeated for the entire length of the line.

line_style is a 16-bit value that specifies the bits of a line that are on or off. By changing the value of the line style, you can change the pattern of lines drawn on your screen.

Example:

```
#include <graph.h>
#include <stdio.h>

main ()
{
    _setvideomode (_MRES16COLOR);
    _setlinestyle (0xF);
    _rectangle (_GBORDER, 0, 0, 50, 50);
    _setlinestyle (0xF0);
    _rectangle (_GBORDER, 60, 0, 110, 50);
    _setlinestyle (0xF0F);
    _rectangle (_GBORDER, 120, 0, 170, 50);
    _setlinestyle (0xCCCC);
    _rectangle (_GBORDER, 180, 0, 230, 50);
    getchar ();
    _setvideomode (_DEFAULTMODE);
}
```

Related Function: _getlinestyle

setmode

int **setmode**(int *file_handle*, int *mode*);

Include file: <fcntl.h> or <io.h>

Description:

setmode sets a file's translation mode to binary mode or text mode.

file_handle is a file handle associated with a file through the creat or open function.

mode specifies the file translation mode. Values and corresponding meanings are as follows:

Value	Meaning
O_TEXT	text or translated mode
O_BINARY	binary mode

If successful, setmode returns the value of the previous translation mode. If an error occurs, setmode returns the value −1 and sets the global variable *errno* to one of the following:

Value	*Meaning*
EBADF	invalid file handle
EINVAL	invalid mode argument

Example:

```
#include <fcntl.h>
#include <io.h>

main()
{
    int old_mode, file_handle;

    if ((file_handle = open("TEST.DAT", O_RDONLY)) == -1)
        printf("Error opening TEST.DAT\n");
    else
        {
        old_mode = setmode(file_handle, O_BINARY);
        if (old_mode == O_TEXT)
            printf("Default mode is text\n");
        else
            printf("Default mode is binary\n");
        close(file_handle);
        }
}
```

Related Functions: creat, fopen, open

_setpixel

short far **_setpixel**(short *x*, short *y*);

Include file: <graph.h>

Description:

_setpixel turns on the pixel at the specified (*x*, *y*) coordinates.

If successful, _setpixel returns the previous pixel value of the specified coordinates. If the coordinates are outside the current clipping region, the routine returns the value −1.

Example:

```
#include <graph.h>
#include <stdio.h>
```

(continued)

```
main()
{
    int x, y;

    _setvideomode(_MRES16COLOR);
    for (x = 10, y = 10; x <= 50; x++, y++)
        {
        _setpixel(x, 10);
        _setpixel(x, 50);
        _setpixel(10, y);
        _setpixel(50, y);
        }
    getchar();
    _setvideomode(_DEFAULTMODE);
}
```

Related Function: _getpixel

_settextcolor

short far **_settextcolor**(short *color*);

Include file: <graph.h>

Description:

_settextcolor sets the color value used for text output by _outtext.

color specifies the desired color using the following values:

Value	Color	Value	Color	Value	Color
0	black	6	brown	12	light red
1	blue	7	white	13	light magenta
2	green	8	dark gray	14	yellow
3	cyan	9	light blue	15	bright white
4	red	10	light green		
5	magenta	11	light cyan		

You can add 16 to a color value to display text in the specified color and enable the blinking attribute.

Example:

```
#include <graph.h>

main()
{
    char buffer[128];
    int color;
```

(continued)

```
        for (color = 0; color < 32; color++)
            {
            _settextcolor(color);
            sprintf(buffer, "Current text color is %d\n",
                    color);
            _outtext(buffer);
            }
}
```

Related Functions: _gettextcolor, _outtext

_settextposition

struct rccoord far **_settextposition**(short *row*, short *column*);

Include file: <graph.h>

Description:

_settextposition sets the beginning row and column position for text output via the _outtext function.

row and *column* specify the desired location for text output to begin.

The include file graph.h defines the structure rccoord as follows:

```
struct rccoord
    {
    short row;
    short column;
    };
```

Upon completion, _settextposition returns the previous text coordinates.

Example:

```
#include <graph.h>

main()
{
    int row, column = 10;
    char buffer[128];

    for (row = 1; row < 10; row++)
        {
        _settextposition(row, column);
        sprintf(buffer, "Row %d, column %d\n",
                row, column);
        _outtext(buffer);
        }
}
```

_settextwindow

void far **_settextwindow**(short *x_left*, short *y_top*,
                          short *x_right*, short *y_bottom*);

Include file: <graph.h>

Description:

_settextwindow specifies the coordinates of the window used for text
output by the _outtext function.

The coordinates (*x_left*, *y_top*) and (*x_right*, *y_bottom*) define the text
window. Text output scrolls up within the window in the same manner
as on the full screen.

Example:

```
#include <graph.h>

main()
{
    int count;
    char buffer[128];

    _settextwindow(10, 20, 20, 60);
    for (count = 0; count < 1000; count++)
        {
        sprintf(buffer, "%d ", count);
        _outtext(buffer);
        }
}
```

Related Functions: _outtext, _settextposition

setvbuf

int **setvbuf**(FILE **file_pointer*, char **buffer*, int *buffer_type*,
       size_t *buffer_size*);

Include file: <stdio.h>

Description:

setvbuf specifies the buffer and buffering technique to be used for
file I/O.

file_pointer is a file pointer associated with a file through an fdopen, fopen, or freopen function.

buffer is a pointer to the file buffer to be used for I/O operations.

buffer_type specifies the buffering technique to be performed. Values and corresponding meanings are as follows:

Value	Meaning
_IOFBF	full buffering
_IOLBF	full buffering (same as _IOFBF)
_IONBF	no buffering

buffer_size is the size of the buffer. Both *buffer* and *buffer_size* are ignored if *buffer_type* is _IONBF.

If the specified buffer points to NULL, setvbuf allocates a buffer whose size equals the specified number of bytes.

If successful, setvbuf returns the value 0. If an error occurs, setvbuf returns a nonzero value.

Example:

```
#include <stdio.h>

main()
{
    char buffer[2048];
    FILE *fp;

    if ((fp = fopen("TEST.DAT", "r")) == NULL)
        printf("Error opening TEST.DAT\n");
    else
        {
        if (setvbuf(fp, buffer, _IOFBF,
                    sizeof(buffer)) != 0)
            printf("Error setting buffer\n");
        else
            /* statements */
        }
}
```

Related Functions: fflush, setbuf

_setvideomode

short far **_setvideomode**(short *video_mode*);

Include file: <graph.h>

Description:

_setvideomode selects the current video-display mode.

video_mode specifies the desired video-display mode. Values and corresponding meanings are as follows:

Value	*Meaning*
_DEFAULTMODE	restores hardware-specific default mode
_ERESNOCOLOR	640 × 350 EGA, 1 color
_ERESCOLOR	640 × 350 EGA, 64 colors
_HERCMONO	Hercules graphics
_HRESBW	640 × 200 CGA, 2 colors
_HRES16COLOR	640 × 200 EGA, 16 colors
_MRES4COLOR	320 × 200 CGA, 4 colors
_MRESNOCOLOR	320 × 200 CGA, 4 colors
_MRES16COLOR	320 × 200 EGA, 16 colors
_MRES256COLOR	320 × 200 VGA, 256 colors
_ORESCOLOR	640 × 400 Olivetti graphics, 1 of 16 colors
_TEXTBW40	40 × 25 CGA, 16 colors
_TEXTC40	40 × 25 CGA, 16 colors
_TEXTBW80	80 × 25 CGA, 16 colors
_TEXTC80	80 × 25 CGA, 16 colors
_TEXTMONO	80 × 25 MDA, 1 color
_VRES2COLOR	640 × 480 VGA, 2 colors
_VRES16COLOR	640 × 480 VGA, 16 colors

Example:

```
#include <graph.h>
#include <stdio.h>

main()
{
    _setvideomode(_MRES16COLOR);
    _rectangle(_GFILLINTERIOR, 50, 50, 200, 200);
    getchar();
    _setvideomode(_DEFAULTMODE);
}
```

Related Function: _getvideoconfig

_setvieworg

struct xycoord far _**setvieworg**(short *x*, short *y*);

Include file: <graph.h>

Description:

_setvieworg moves the origin (0, 0) of the view coordinates used by the graphics routines to the specified physical-device coordinates.

The include file graph.h defines the structure xycoord as follows:

```
struct xycoord
    {
    short xcoord;
    short ycoord;
    };
```

Upon completion, _setvieworg returns the previous physical coordinates of the view origin.

Example:

```
#include <graph.h>
#include <stdio.h>

main()
{
    _setvideomode(_MRES16COLOR);
    _setvieworg(100, 100);
    _rectangle(_GFILLINTERIOR, 0, 0, 50, 50);
    _setvieworg(0, 0);
    _rectangle(_GBORDER, 0, 0, 50, 50);
    getchar();
    _setvideomode(_DEFAULTMODE);
}
```

Related Functions: _setcliprgn, _setviewport

_setviewport

void far _**setviewport**(short *x_left*, short *y_top*,
                          short *x_right*, short *y_bottom*);

Include file: <graph.h>

Description:

_setviewport defines a clipping region on the graphics screen and then sets the origin of the view coordinates to the upper-left corner of the region.

The coordinates (x_left, y_top) and (x_right, y_bottom) define the graphics viewport.

Example:

```
#include <graph.h>
#include <stdio.h>

main()
{
    _setvideomode(_MRES16COLOR);
    _setviewport(50, 50, 200, 200);
    _rectangle(_GFILLINTERIOR, 0, 0, 80, 80);
    getchar();
    _setvideomode(_DEFAULTMODE);
}
```

Related Functions: _setcliprgn, _setvieworg

_setvisualpage

short far **_setvisualpage**(short *video_page*);

Include file: <graph.h>

Description:

_setvisualpage selects which video-display page is to be visible on the screen.

The routine _setactivepage selects the video-display page to which graphics output is to be written. _setvisualpage allows you to display the active page.

The available number of video-display pages will differ according to your hardware configuration.

Example: See _setactivepage.

Related Functions: _setactivepage, _setvideomode

signal

void (*signal(int *event*, void(*function*)(int *event* [,int *subcode*])))
    (int *event*);

Include file: <signal.h>

Description:

signal specifies a program-defined function to serve as an interrupt handler.

event specifies the signal to be trapped. Values and corresponding meanings are as follows:

Value	Meaning
SIGABRT	program termination with an exit status of 3
SIGFPE	floating-point error
SIGILL	illegal instruction
SIGINT	interrupt 0x23 (ctrl+C)
SIGSEGV	illegal storage access
SIGTERM	termination request

function is either the name of the handler routine or one of the following constant values:

Value	Meaning
SIG_DFL	performs default handling
SIG_IGN	ignores signal
SIG_ERR	ignores signal (OS/2 only)
SIG_ACK	acknowledges signal (OS/2 only)

subcode is an optional error code.

Example: See raise.

Related Functions: abort, exit, raise

sin, sinh

double **sin**(double *expression*);

or

double **sinh**(double *expression*);

Include file: <math.h>

Description:

sin returns the sine of a numeric expression; sinh returns the hyperbolic sine of a numeric expression.

expression is a double-precision expression that specifies an angle in radians.

Example:

```
#include <math.h>

main()
{
    double radians;

    for (radians = 0.0; radians < 4.0; radians += 0.1)
        printf("Sine of %f is %f\n",
                radians, sin(radians));
}
```

Related Functions: acos, cos, tan

---

sopen

int **sopen**(char *pathname*, int *mode*, int *share_access*[, int *permission*]);

Include files: <fcntl.h>, <sys\types.h>, <sys\stat.h>, <share.h>, and <io.h>

Description:

sopen opens and prepares a file for shared read and write operations.

pathname is a character string that specifies the pathname of the file to be opened.

mode specifies how the program will access the file. Valid values are as follows:

O_APPEND, O_BINARY, O_CREAT, O_EXCL, O_RDONLY, O_RDWR, O_TEXT, O_TRUNC, O_WRONLY

Also see open.

share_access specifies the supported file-sharing operations. Values and corresponding meanings are as follows:

Value	Meaning
SH_COMPAT	compatibility mode
SH_DENYRW	denies read and write access
SH_DENYWR	denies write access
SH_DENYRD	denies read access
SH_DENYNO	allows read and write access

permission specifies file-access permissions when the sopen function creates a file.

Value	Meaning
S_IWRITE	write access
S_IREAD	read access
S_IWRITE ¦ S_IREAD	read and write access

If successful, sopen returns a file handle. If an error occurs, sopen returns the value −1 and sets the global variable *errno* to one of the following values:

Value	Meaning
EACCES	access violation
EEXIST	sopen specifies O_CREAT and O_EXCL, and the specified file already exists
EMFILE	too many files
ENOENT	file not found

Example:

```
#include <fcntl.h>
#include <sys\types.h>
#include <sys\stat.h>
#include <share.h>
#include <io.h>

main()
{
    int handle;

    if ((handle = sopen("TEST.DAT", O_RDONLY,
                        SH_DENYWR)) == -1)
        printf("Error accessing TEST.DAT\n");
    else
        /* statements */
}
```

Related Functions: creat, open, umask

spawnl

int **spawnl**(int *invoke_flag*, char **pathname*, char **arg0*, ...,
        char **argn*, NULL);

Include file: <process.h> or <stdlib.h>

Description:

spawnl executes a specified DOS command by using a null-terminated
list of arguments. When the command completes execution, the program resumes control.

spawnl is similar to execl except that spawnl returns control to the
program when it completes the specified DOS command.

invoke_flag specifies how spawnl executes the command. Values and
corresponding meanings are as follows:

Value	Meaning
P_WAIT	suspends program execution until the spawned program completes
P_NOWAIT	continues to execute concurrently with the spawned program
P_OVERLAY	overlays the current program in memory with the spawned program. Same effect as using execl

arg0 to *argn* are pointers to character strings that contain the program's command-line arguments.

spawnl does not support the PATH environment entry.

Example:

```
#include <process.h>
#include <stdio.h>

main()
{
    spawnl(P_WAIT, "TEST.EXE", "TEST", NULL);
    printf("Control back to program\n");
    getchar();
}
```

Related Functions: spawnle, spawnlp, spawnlpe, spawnv, spawnve,
spawnvp, spawnvpe

spawnle

int **spawnle**(int *invoke_flag*, char **pathname*, char **arg0*, ...,
        char **argn*, NULL, char **env*[]);

Include file: <process.h> or <stdlib.h>

Description:

spawnle executes a specified DOS command by using a null-terminated list of arguments and an array of pointers to the environment entries. When the command completes execution, the program resumes control.

spawnle is identical to spawnl except that spawnle allows you to specify the environment entries for the command.

Example:

```
#include <process.h>
#include <stdio.h>

main()
{
    static char *env[] = {"A=AAA", "B=BBB", NULL};

    spawnle(P_WAIT, "TEST.EXE", "TEST", "A", "B",
            NULL, env);
    printf("Back in program\n");
    getchar();
}
```

Related Functions: spawnl, spawnlp, spawnlpe, spawnv, spawnve, spawnvp, spawnvpe

---

spawnlp

int **spawnlp**(int *invoke_flag*, char **pathname*, char **arg0*, ...,
        char **argn, NULL);*

Include file: <process.h> or <stdlib.h>

Description:

spawnlp executes a specified DOS command by using a null-terminated list of arguments. When the command completes execution, the program resumes control.

spawnlp is identical to spawnl except that spawnlp supports the DOS PATH environment entry.

Example: See spawnl.

Related Functions: spawnl, spawnle, spawnlpe, spawnv, spawnve, spawnvp, spawnvpe

spawnlpe

int **spawnlpe**(int *invoke_flag*, char *∗pathname*, char *∗arg0*, ..., char *∗argn*, NULL, char *∗env*[]);

Include file: <process.h> or <stdlib.h>

Description:

spawnlpe executes a specified DOS command by using a null-terminated list of arguments and an array of pointers to the environment entries. When the command completes execution, the program resumes control.

spawnlpe is identical to spawnle except that spawnlpe supports the DOS PATH environment entry.

Example: See spawnle.

Related Functions: spawnl, spawnle, spawnlp, spawnv, spawnve, spawnvp, spawnvpe

spawnv

int **spawnv**(int *invoke_flag*, char *∗pathname*, char *∗argv*[]);

Include file: <process.h> or <stdlib.h>

Description:

spawnv executes a specified DOS command by using an array of pointers to the command-line arguments. When the command completes execution, the program resumes control.

spawnv is identical to spawnl except that spawnv uses an array of character-string pointers to the command-line arguments.

spawnv does not support the PATH environment entry.

Example:

```
#include <process.h>
#include <stdio.h>

main()
{
    static char *args[] = {"TEST", "TEST.EXE", "A",
                           "B", "C", NULL};

    spawnv(P_WAIT, "TEST.EXE", args);
    printf("Back in program\n");
    getchar();
}
```

Related Functions: spawnl, spawnle, spawnlp, spawnlpe, spawnve, spawnvp, spawnvpe

---

spawnve

int **spawnve**(int *invoke_flag*, char **pathname*, char **argv*[],
        char **env*[]);

Include file: <process.h> or <stdlib.h>

Description:

spawnve executes a specified DOS command by using an array of pointers to the command-line arguments and an array of pointers to the environment entries. When the command completes execution, the program resumes control.

spawnve is identical to spawnle except that spawnv uses an array of character-string pointers to the command-line arguments.

spawnve does not support the PATH environment entry.

Example:

```
#include <process.h>
#include <stdio.h>

main()
{
    static char *args[] = {"TEST", "TEST.EXE", "A",
                           "B", "C", NULL};
    static char *env[] = {"A=AAA", "B=BBB", NULL};

    spawnve(P_WAIT, "TEST.EXE", args, env);
    printf("Back in program\n");
    getchar();
}
```

Related Functions: spawnl, spawnle, spawnlp, spawnlpe, spawnv, spawnvp, spawnvpe

spawnvp

int **spawnvp**(int *invoke_flag*, char *pathname*, char *argv[]);

Include file: <process.h> or <stdlib.h>

Description:

spawnvp executes a specified DOS command by using an array of pointers to the command-line arguments. When the command completes execution, the program resumes control.

spawnvp is similar to spawnv except that spawnvp supports the DOS PATH environment entry.

Example: See spawnv.

Related Functions: spawnl, spawnle, spawnlp, spawnlpe, spawnv, spawnve, spawnvpe

spawnvpe

int **spawnvpe**(int *invoke_flag*, char *pathname*, char *argv[],
            char *env[]);

Include file: <process.h> or <stdlib.h>

Description:

spawnvpe executes a specified DOS command by using an array of pointers to the command-line arguments and an array of pointers to the environment entries. When the command completes execution, the program resumes control.

spawnvpe is identical to spawnve except that spawnvpe supports the DOS PATH environment entry.

Example: See spawnve.

Related Functions: spawnl, spawnle, spawnlp, spawnlpe, spawnv, spawnve, spawnvp

_splitpath

void **_splitpath**(char *pathname*, char *drive*, char *subdirectory*,
char **filename*, char *extension*);

Include file: <stdlib.h>

Description:

_splitpath breaks down a complete pathname into a disk-drive letter, a subdirectory path, a filename, and an extension.

The include file stdlib.h defines the constants _MAX_DRIVE, _MAX_DIR, _MAX_FNAME, and _MAX_EXT, which specify the buffer size for each pathname component.

pathname is a character string that contains the complete pathname to be broken down.

drive is the disk-drive letter followed by a colon (or an empty string if the pathname did not include a disk-drive letter).

subdirectory is a character string that contains the complete subdirectory path to the file (or an empty string if the pathname did not specify a subdirectory path).

filename is a character string that contains the filename (or an empty string if no filename was specified).

extension is a character string that contains the extension (or an empty string if no extension was specified).

Example:

```
#include <stdlib.h>

main()
{
    char drive[_MAX_DRIVE], sub[_MAX_DIR];
    char filename[_MAX_FNAME], ext[_MAX_EXT];

    _splitpath("A:\\DOS\\DISKCOPY.COM", drive, sub,
               filename, ext);
    printf("Drive %s\t Subdirectory %s\n", drive, sub);
    printf("Filename %s\t Extension %s\n", filename, ext);
}
```

This program produces the following result:

```
Drive A:          Subdirectory \DOS\
Filename DISKCOPY          Extension .COM
```

Related Function: _makepath

sprintf

int **sprintf**(char *buffer*, char *format_specification*[, *argument*] ...);

Include file: <stdio.h>

Description:

sprintf formats a sequence of characters and stores it in a character-string buffer.

buffer is a character-string buffer in which the characters are placed.

format_specification is a character string that specifies the output format of the characters. All format specifiers supported by printf are valid.

argument is an optional expression to be formatted and stored in the string.

Example:

```
#include <stdio.h>

main()
{
    char buffer[128];

    sprintf(buffer, "%d + %d = %d", 1, 1, 1 + 1);
    puts(buffer);
    sprintf(buffer, "%d is the previous result\n",
            1 + 1);
    puts(buffer);
}
```

Related Functions: printf, sscanf

sqrt

double **sqrt**(double *expression*);

Include file: <math.h>

Description:

sqrt returns the square root of a specified numeric expression.

expression is any numeric expression greater than or equal to 0.

If the expression is negative, sqrt returns the value 0, sends an error message to stderr, and sets the global variable *errno* to the value EDOM.

Example:

```
#include <math.h>

main()
{
    double i;

    for (i = 0; i <= 25; i += 1.0)
        printf("The square root of %f is %f\n",
                i, sqrt(i));
}
```

srand

void **srand**(unsigned *seed*);

Include file: <stdlib.h>

Description:

srand uses a specified seed to assign a starting value to the random-number generator.

A seed of 1 resets the random-number generator.

Example:

```
#include <stdlib.h>

main()
{
    int i;

    for (i = 0; i < 5; i++)
        printf("%d\n", rand());
    srand(555);
    for (i = 0; i < 5; i++)
        printf("%d\n", rand());
    srand(1);
    for (i = 0; i < 5; i++)
        printf("%d\n", rand());
}
```

Related Function: rand

sscanf

int **sscanf**(char *buffer*, char *format_specification*[, *argument*] ...);

Include file: <stdio.h>

Description:

sscanf reads data from a character string (as opposed to an input device or file) into the specified variables.

buffer is the character-string buffer from which characters are read.

format_specification is a character string that specifies the input format. All format specifiers supported by scanf are valid.

argument is a pointer to a variable to which sscanf assigns a value.

If successful, sscanf returns a count of the number of variables to which it assigned values. If you attempt to read past the end of a string, sscanf returns the value EOF.

Example:

```
#include <stdio.h>

main()
{
    static char *buffer = "1 2.2 3";
    int a, c;
    float b;

    sscanf(buffer, "%d %f %d", &a, &b, &c);
    printf("%d %f %d\n", a, b, c);
}
```

Related Functions: scanf, sprintf

stackavail

size_t **stackavail**(void);

Include file: <malloc.h>

Description:

stackavail returns an approximation of the number of available bytes of stack space.

The /F option of the CL and QCL commands allows you to specify the amount of stack space to be allocated for your program.

Example:

```
#include <malloc.h>

main()
{
    printf("In main: %u\n", stackavail());
    function(1, 2, 3);
}

function(int a, int b, int c)
{
    printf("In function: %u\n", stackavail());
}
```

This program produces the following result:

```
In main: 1766
In function: 1756
```

Related Functions: alloca, _memavl

---

stat

int **stat**(char *pathname*, struct stat *file_info*);

Include files: <sys\types.h> and <sys\stat.h>

Description:

stat returns information about the specified file.

pathname is a character string that contains the pathname of the desired file.

file_info is a pointer to a structure of type stat defined in the include file stat.h as follows:

```
struct stat
    {
    dev_t st_dev;                /* drive number or
                                    device handle */
    ino_t st_ino;                /* not used by DOS */
    unsigned short st_mode;      /* file mode bit mask */
    short st_nlink;              /* always 1 */
    short st_uid;                /* not used by DOS */
    short st_gid;                /* not used by DOS */
    dev_t st_rdev;               /* same as st_dev */
    off_t st_size;               /* size in bytes */
    time_t st_atime;             /* modification date */
    time_t st_mtime;             /* same as st_atime */
    time_t st_ctime;             /* same as st_atime */
    };
```

If successful, stat returns the value 0. If an error occurs, stat returns the value −1 and sets the global variable *errno* to the value ENOENT.

Example:

```
#include <sys\types.h>
#include <sys\stat.h>
#include <time.h>

main(int argc, char *argv[])
{
    struct stat fileinfo;

    if (stat(argv[1], &fileinfo) == -1)
        printf("Error accessing %s\n", argv[1]);
    else
        {
        printf("File: %s  Size: %u  Drive: %d\n",
                argv[1], fileinfo.st_size,
                fileinfo.st_dev);
        printf("Date last modified: %s\n",
                ctime(&fileinfo.st_mtime));
        }
}
```

Related Functions: access, fstat

_status87

unsigned int **_status87**(void);

Include file: <float.h> or <math.h>

Description:

_status87 returns the floating-point status word.

See _clear87 for status values and corresponding meanings.

Example:

```
#include <float.h>

main()
{
    printf("Current floating-point status: %x\n",
            _status87);
}
```

Related Functions: _clear87, _control87

strcat

char *__strcat__(char *_target_, char *_source_);

Include file: <string.h>

Description:

strcat appends one string (_source_) to another string (_target_).

Example:

```
#include <string.h>

main()
{
    static char target[128] = "Start of";
    static char source[128] = " the string";

    strcat(target, source);
    puts(target);
}
```

This program produces the following result:

```
Start of the string
```

__Related Functions:__ strcpy, strdup, strncat, strncpy

strchr

char *__strchr__(char *_string_, int _letter_);

Include file: <string.h>

Description:

strchr searches a string for the first occurrence of a specified character.

string is the character string to be searched for the specified character.

letter is the ASCII character for which to search.

If successful, strchr returns a pointer to the first occurrence of the specified character. If the character is not found, strchr returns the value NULL.

Example:

```
#include <string.h>
#include <stdio.h>

main()
{
    char letter = 'Z';
    static char *str = "ABCDEFZ";
    char *ptr;

    ptr = strchr(str, letter);
    if (*ptr != NULL)
        printf("Letter found at address %p\n", ptr);
    else
        printf("Letter not found\n");
}
```

Related Functions: strrchr, strstr

strcmp

int **strcmp**(char *s1, char *s2);

Include file: <string.h>

Description:

strcmp compares the characters of two strings.

strcmp compares the strings on a character-by-character basis. If a character in the first string is greater than the corresponding character in the second string, strcmp returns a negative value. If the two character strings are identical, strcmp returns the value 0. If a character in the second string is greater than the corresponding character in the first string, strcmp returns the value 1.

Example:

```
#include <string.h>

main()
{
    printf("Comparing AAA with aaa: %d\n",
            strcmp("AAA", "aaa"));
    printf("Comparing AAA with AAA: %d\n",
            strcmp("AAA", "AAA"));
    printf("Comparing aaa with AAA: %d\n",
            strcmp("aaa", "AAA"));
}
```

This program produces the following result:

```
Comparing AAA with aaa: -1
Comparing AAA with AAA: 0
Comparing aaa with AAA: 1
```

Related Functions: strcmpi, stricmp

strcmpi

int **strcmpi**(char *s1, char *s2);

Include file: <string.h>

Description:

strcmpi compares two strings without regard to case.

strcmpi is identical to strcmp except that strcmpi is case-insensitive.

Example:

```
#include <string.h>

main()
{
    printf("Comparing AAA with aaa: %d\n",
            strcmpi("AAA", "aaa"));
    printf("Comparing AAA with AAA: %d\n",
            strcmpi("AAA", "AAA"));
}
```

This program produces the following result:

```
Comparing AAA with aaa: 0
Comparing AAA with AAA: 0
```

Related Functions: strcmp, stricmp

strcpy

char ***strcpy**(char *target, char *source);

Include file: <string.h>

Description:

strcpy copies the contents of one character string into another character string.

target is a character string into which the source string is to be copied.
source is a character string to be copied.

Example:

```
#include <string.h>

main()
{
    char *source = "String to copy";
    char target[128];

    strcpy(target, source);
    puts(target);
}
```

Related Function: strdup

strcspn

size_t **strcspn**(char *string*, char *characters*);

Include file: <string.h>

Description:

strcspn searches a string for all specified characters.

If successful, strcspn returns the index of the first character in *string* that belongs to the set of characters specified in *characters*. If none of the characters is found, strcspn returns the length of the string.

Example:

```
#include <string.h>
#include <stdio.h>

main()
{
    int offset;
    static char str[128] = "ABCDEF";

    offset = strcspn(str, "ED");
    if (offset != strlen(str))
        printf("Character found at offset %d\n", offset);
    else
        printf("Character not found\n");
}
```

Related Function: strspn

_strdate

char *__strdate__(char *_buffer_);

Include file: <time.h>

Description:

_strdate assigns the current system date to a character-string buffer.

buffer is a character-string buffer to which _strdate assigns the date in the format _mm/dd/yy_.

Example:

```
#include <time.h>

main()
{
    char date[9];

    _strdate(date);
    printf("Current system date is %s\n", date);
}
```

This program produces the following result:

```
Current system date is 01/08/89
```

Related Function: _strtime

strdup

char *__strdup__(char *_source_);

Include file: <string.h>

Description:

strdup allocates storage space (with a call to malloc) for a copy of a string and copies the contents of the source string to the space.

source is a character string to be copied.

If successful, strdup returns a pointer to the duplicated string. If strdup cannot allocate the specified amount of memory, strdup returns the value NULL.

Example:

```
#include <string.h>

main()
{
    static char *source = "String to duplicate";
    char *target;

    if (target = strdup(source))
        puts(target);
    else
        printf("Error duplicating source\n");
}
```

Related Function: strcpy

stricmp

int **stricmp**(char ∗*s1*, char ∗*s2*);

Include file: <string.h>

Description:

stricmp compares two character strings without regard to case. stricmp is identical to strcmpi.

Example: See strcmpi.

Related Functions: strcmp, strcmpi

strerror

char ∗**strerror**(int *error_number*);

Include file: <string.h>

Description:

strerror returns the error message that corresponds to the specified error number.

error_number is usually the value of the global variable *errno*.

Example:

```
#include <stdlib.h>
#include <string.h>

main()
{
    int i;

    for (i = 0; i <= sys_nerr; i++)
        puts(strerror(i));
}
```

Related Functions: clearerr, perror, _strerror

_strerror

char *_strerror(char *str);

Include file: <string.h>

Description:

_strerror returns a character string that contains the error message associated with the current value of the global variable *errno*.

If the character string passed to _strerror is NULL, _strerror returns a character string that contains only the error message that corresponds to *errno*. If the string is not NULL, _strerror returns a character string that contains the characters of the string followed by the error message corresponding to *errno*.

Example:

```
#include <string.h>
#include <stdio.h>

main()
{
    FILE *fp;

    if ((fp = fopen("XXXX.YYY", "r")) == NULL)
        {
        puts(_strerror(NULL));
        puts(_strerror("Can't open the file"));
        }
}
```

Related Functions: clearerr, perror, strerror

strlen

int **strlen**(char ∗*str*);

Include file: <string.h>

Description:

strlen returns in bytes the length of a specified null-terminated character string.

str is a character string whose length is to be returned. The strlen function does not include the NULL character in its character count.

Example:

```
#include <string.h>
#include <stdio.h>

main()
{
    static char *str = "This is a test";
    int i, length;

    length = strlen(str);
    printf("%s contains %d characters\n", str, length);
    for (i = 0; i < length; i++)
        putchar(str[i]);
}
```

strlwr

char ∗**strlwr**(char ∗*str*);

Include file: <string.h>

Description:

strlwr converts the uppercase letters of a character string to lowercase letters.

str is a character string to be converted to a lowercase string.

Example:

```
#include <stdio.h>
#include <string.h>
```

(continued)

```
main(int argc, char *argv[])
{
    /* display a file in lowercase */
    FILE *fp;
    char buffer[128];

    if ((fp = fopen(argv[1], "r")) == NULL)
        printf("Error opening %s\n", argv[1]);
    else
        {
        while (fgets(buffer, sizeof(buffer), fp))
            fputs(strlwr(buffer), stdout);
        fclose(fp);
        }
}
```

Related Function: strupr

strncat

char *__strncat__(char *_target_, char *_source_, size_t _num_bytes_);

Include file: <string.h>

Description:

strncat appends _num_bytes_ characters of a source string to a specified target string.

target is a character string to which characters are to be appended.

source is a character string from which characters are to be copied.

_num_bytes_ specifies the number of characters to be copied from the source string and appended to the target string. If the number of bytes exceeds the number of characters in the string, strncat copies only the characters up to, and including, the NULL character.

Example:

```
#include <string.h>
#include <stdio.h>

main()
{
    char target[128];
    static char *source = "ABCDEF";
    int i;
```

(continued)

```
    target[0] = NULL;
    for (i = 1; i <= 6; i++)
        {
        strncat(target, source, i);
        puts(target);
        }
}
```

This program produces the following result:

```
A
AAB
AABABC
AABABCABCD
AABABCABCDABCDE
AABABCABCDABCDEABCDEF
```

Related Function: strcat

strncmp

int **strncmp**(char *s1, char *s2, size_t *num_bytes*);

Include file: <string.h>

Description:

strncmp compares the first *num_bytes* bytes of two character strings.

strncmp is identical to strcmp except that strncmp compares only the first *num_bytes* characters of two character strings. Also see strcmp.

Example:

```
#include <string.h>

main()
{
    char *s1 = "AAAAF";
    char *s2 = "AAABC";
    int i;

    for (i = 1; i <= 5; i++)
        printf("Comparing %d characters; result: %d\n",
                i, strncmp(s1, s2, i));
}
```

Related Function: strcmp

strncpy

char ***strncpy**(char *target*, char *source*, int *num_bytes*);

Include file: <string.h>

Description:

strncpy copies the first *num_bytes* characters from a source string to a target string.

target is a character string to which the characters are to be copied.

source is a character string that contains the characters to be copied.

num_bytes specifies the number of characters to be copied.

Example:

```
#include <string.h>
#include <stdio.h>

main()
{
    char target[128];
    char *source = "ABCDEFGHI";
    int i;

    for (i = 1; i <= 10; i++)
        {
        strncpy(target, source, i);
        target[i] = NULL;
        puts(target);
        }
}
```

Related Function: strcpy

strnicmp

int **strnicmp**(char *s1*, char *s2*, int *num_bytes*);

Include file: <string.h>

Description:

strnicmp compares the first *num_bytes* characters of two character strings without regard to case.

strnicmp is identical to strncmp except that strnicmp is case-insensitive. Also see stricmp.

Example:

```
#include <string.h>

main()
{
    char *s1 = "AAABC";
    char *s2 = "aAaDB";
    int i;

    for (i = 1; i <= 5; i++)
        printf("Comparing %d characters; result: %d\n",
                i, strnicmp(s1, s2, i));
}
```

Related Functions: strcmp, strncmp

strnset

char *__strnset__(char *string, int letter, size_t num_bytes);

Include file: <string.h>

Description:

strnset assigns the specified character to the first num_bytes characters of a string.

string is a character string to which the characters are to be assigned.

letter is a character to be assigned to the string.

num_bytes specifies the number of characters to be assigned to the string.

Example:

```
#include <string.h>
#include <stdio.h>

main()
{
    char buffer[128];
    int i;

    for (i = 10; i >= 1; i==)
        {
        strnset(buffer, 'A', i);
```

(continued)

```
        buffer[i] = NULL;
        puts(buffer);
        }
}
```

Related Function: memset

---

strpbrk

char *__strpbrk__(char *_s1_, char *_s2_);

Include file: <string.h>

Description:

strpbrk returns a pointer to the first occurrence in the first string of any character that is contained in the second string.

If strpbrk locates within the first string a character from the second string, it returns a pointer to the character. If no matching characters are found, strpbrk returns the value NULL.

Example:

```
#include <string.h>
#include <stdio.h>

main()
{
    char *s1 = "Test string";
    char *s2 = "st";

    printf("Searching %s for %s; result: %d\n", s1, s2,
        strpbrk(s1, s2) - s1);
}
```

---

strrchr

char *__strrchr__(const char *_str_, int _letter_);

Include file: <string.h>

Description:

strrchr returns a pointer to the rightmost occurrence of a specified character within a string.

str is a character string to be searched for a specified character.

letter is an ASCII character for which to search.

If strrchr successfully locates the character, it returns a pointer to the rightmost occurrence of the character. If strrchr does not locate the character, it returns the value NULL.

Example:

```
#include <string.h>

main()
{
    char *ptr;

    ptr = strrchr("This is a test", 'a');
    if (*ptr)
        printf("Rightmost s is at %p\n", ptr);
    else
        printf("Letter s was not found\n");
}
```

Related Function: strchr

strrev

char *strrev(char *str);

Include file: <string.h>

Description:

strrev reverses the order of characters within a string.

str is a character string whose order is to be reversed.

Example:

```
#include <string.h>

main()
{
    char *str = "ABCDEF";
    strrev(str);
    puts(str);
}
```

strset

char *strset(char *str, int letter);

Include file: <string.h>

Description:

strset sets to a specified character all characters in a string up to the NULL character.

str is a character string to which a specified character is to be assigned.

letter is an ASCII character to be assigned to a specified character string.

Example:

```
#include <string.h>

main()
{
    static char *a = "A", *b = "BB", *c = "CCC";

    strset(a, 'a');
    strset(b, 'b');
    strset(c, 'c');
    printf("%s %s %s\n", a, b, c);
}
```

This program produces the following result:

```
a bb ccc
```

Related Function: strnset

strspn

size_t strspn(const char *s1, const char *s2);

Include file: <string.h>

Description:

strspn returns the index position of the first character in the first string that is not in the second string.

s1 is a string to be searched for characters contained in *s2*. If all characters in the first string (*s1*) appear in the second (*s2*), strspn returns an integer value equal to the length of the first string.

Example:

```
#include <string.h>

main()
{
    char *s1 = "abc";
    char *s2 = "ab";
    int index;

    index = strspn(s1, s2);
    printf("First character that differs:\n");
    printf("%c at offset %d\n", s1[index], index);
}
```

Related Function: strcspn

strstr

char *strstr(const char *string*, const char *substring*);

Include file: <string.h>

Description:

strstr returns a pointer to the first occurrence of a substring within a string.

string is a character string to be searched for a specified substring.

substring is the character string for which to search.

If successful, strstr returns a pointer to the first occurrence of the substring. If the substring is not found, strstr returns the value NULL.

Example:

```
#include <string.h>

main()
{
    char *str = "This is a test";
    char *substring = "is";
    char *loc;

    loc = strstr(str, substring);
```

(continued)

```
    if (*loc)
        printf("First occurrence of %s in %s",
               substring, str);
        printf(" is offset %d\n", loc - str);
    else
        printf("%s not found in %s\n", substring, str);
}
```

Related Function: strcspn

_strtime

char *_**strtime**(char *time);

Include file: <time.h>

Description:

_strtime assigns the current system time to the specified character-string buffer.

time is a character-string buffer to which the system time is assigned in the format *hh:mm:ss*.

Example:

```
#include <time.h>

main()
{
    char time[9];

    _strtime(time);
    printf("Current system time is %s\n", time);
}
```

Related Functions: asctime, ctime, _strdate, time

strtod

double **strtod**(const char *str, char **endscan);

Include file: <stdlib.h>

Description:

strtod converts a character-string representation of a value to a double-precision value.

str is a character string to be converted.

endscan is a pointer to the character responsible for ending the conversion. If *endscan* is NULL, strtod used all the characters in the string during the conversion.

If successful, strtod returns a double-precision value. If overflow occurs, strtod returns the value HUGE_VAL and sets the global variable *errno* to the value ERANGE. If the value cannot be converted, or if underflow occurs, strtod returns the value 0.

Example:

```
#include <stdlib.h>

main()
{
    char *good_val = "1.23456";
    char *bad_val = "1.23XYZ";
    char *endscan;
    double result;

    result = strtod(good_val, &endscan);
    printf("%f %s %s\n", result, good_val, endscan);
    result = strtod(bad_val, &endscan);
    printf("%f %s %s\n", result, bad_val, endscan);
}
```

Related Functions: strtol, strtoul

strtok

char *__strtok__(char *__str__, const char *__tokens__);

Include file: <string.h>

Description:

strtok returns a pointer to the location of a token in a string.

str is a character string to be searched for tokens. If the string is NULL, strtok uses the ending location of the previous string.

tokens is a character string containing the tokens for which to search.

If successful, strtok returns a pointer to the token position. If no tokens are found, strtok returns the value NULL.

Example:

```
#include <string.h>
#include <stdio.h>
```

(continued)

```
main()
{
    char *str = "10, 20, 30, 40, 50";
    char *token = ",";
    char *ptr;

    ptr = strtok(str, token);
    while (*str)
        {
        if (ptr)
            {
            while (str != ptr)
                if (*str)
                    putchar(*str++);
                else
                    str++;
            }
        else
            while (*str)
                putchar(*str++);
        putchar('\n');
        ptr = strtok(NULL, token);
        }
}
```

strtol

long **strtol**(char *str, char **endscan, int base);

Include file: <stdlib.h>

Description:

strtol converts a character-string representation of a value to a long-integer value.

str is a character string to be converted.

endscan is a pointer to the character responsible for ending the conversion. If endscan is NULL, strtol used all the characters in the string during the conversion.

base is the numeric base to be used for the conversion. The value 2 is binary, 8 is octal, 10 is decimal, 16 is hexadecimal, and so on.

If successful, strtol returns a long-integer value. If the value cannot be converted, strtol returns the value 0. If overflow occurs, strtol returns the value LONG_MAX or LONG_MIN, depending on the sign of the value, and sets the global variable errno to the value ERANGE.

Example:

```
#include <stdlib.h>

main()
{
    long result;
    char *good_val = "1001";
    char *bad_val = "10XX";
    char *endscan;

    result = strtol(good_val, &endscan, 10);
    printf("%ld %s %s Base 10\n", result,
            good_val, endscan);
    result = strtol(good_val, &endscan, 2);
    printf("%ld %s %s Base 2\n", result,
            good_val, endscan);
    result = strtol(bad_val, &endscan, 10);
    printf("%ld %s %s Base 10\n", result,
            bad_val, endscan);
}
```

Related Functions: strtod, strtoul

strtoul

unsigned long **strtoul**(char *str, char **endscan, int base);

Include file: <stdlib.h>

Description:

strtoul converts a character-string representation of a value to an unsigned long-integer value.

str is a character string to be converted.

endscan is a pointer to the character responsible for ending the conversion. If *endscan* is NULL, strtoul used all the characters in the string during the conversion.

base is the numeric base to be used for the conversion. The value 2 is binary, 8 is octal, 10 is decimal, 16 is hexadecimal, and so on.

If successful, strtoul returns an unsigned long-integer value. If the string cannot be converted, strtoul returns the value 0. If overflow occurs, strtoul returns the value ULONG_MAX and sets the global variable *errno* to the value ERANGE.

Example:

```
#include <stdlib.h>

main()
{
    char *good_val = "12345";
    char *bad_val = "12X345";
    char *endscan;
    unsigned long result;

    result = strtoul(good_val, &endscan, 10);
    printf("%ld %s %s Base 10\n", result,
            good_val, endscan);
    result = strtoul(bad_val, &endscan, 10);
    printf("%ld %s %s Base 10\n", result,
            bad_val, endscan);
}
```

Related Functions: strtod, strtol

strupr

char *__strupr__(char *str);

Include file: <string.h>

Description:

strupr converts the lowercase characters of a string to uppercase characters.

str is a character string to be converted to an uppercase string.

Example:

```
#include <string.h>

main()
{
    char *str = "String oF lettERS";

    printf("%s\n", strupr(str));
}
```

This program produces the following result:

```
STRING OF LETTERS
```

Related Function: strlwr

swab

void **swab**(char *source*, char *target*, int *num_bytes*);

Include file: <stdlib.h>

Description:

swab copies *num_bytes* bytes from a source string, swaps each pair of adjacent bytes, and stores the result in a target buffer.

The swab function is typically used to prepare binary data for transfer to a machine that uses a different byte order.

source is a buffer that contains the original data.

target is a buffer to which the swapped bytes are to be copied.

num_bytes specifies the number of bytes to be copied and swapped.

system

int **system**(const char *command*);

Include file: <stdlib.h> or <process.h>

Description:

system executes a specified operating-system command.

command is a character string that contains the command to be executed.

If successful, system returns the value 0. If an error occurs, system returns the value −1 and sets the global variable *errno* to one of the following:

Value	Meaning
E2BIG	argument string exceeds 128 bytes
ENOENT	could not locate COMMAND.COM
ENOEXEC	invalid COMMAND.COM
ENOMEM	insufficient memory

Example:

```
#include <process.h>
```

(continued)

```
main()
{
    system("DIR");
}
```

Related Functions: execl, execle, execlp, execlpe, execv, execve, execvp, execvpe, spawnl, spawnle, spawnlp, spawnlpe, spawnv, spawnve, spawnvp, spawnvpe

tan, tanh

double **tan**(double *expression*);

or

double **tanh**(double *expression*);

Include file: <math.h>

Description:

tan returns the tangent of a numeric expression; tanh returns the hyperbolic tangent of a numeric expression.

expression is a double-precision expression that specifies an angle in radians.

Example:

```
#include <math.h>

main()
{
    printf("Tangent of pi/4 is %f\n",
            tan(3.14159265 / 4));
}
```

Related Functions: acos, asin, atan, atan2, cos, cosh, sin, sinh

tell

long **tell**(int *file_handle*);

Include file: <io.h>

Description:

tell returns the current file-pointer offset for the file associated with the specified handle.

file_handle is a file handle associated with a file through the creat or open function.

If successful, tell returns the current file-pointer offset. If an error occurs, tell returns the value −1 and sets the global variable *errno* to the value EBADF.

Example:

```
#include <io.h>

main()
{
    long position;
    int file_handle;

    /* statements */
    position = tell(file_handle);
    /* statements */
}
```

Related Functions: ftell, lseek

tempnam

char *tempnam(char *directory*, char *prefix*);

Include file: <stdio.h>

Description:

tempnam generates a unique filename in the subdirectory defined by the environment entry TMP or in the specified subdirectory.

directory specifies the name of the subdirectory in which the file is to be created if the TMP entry does not exist or the subdirectory it specifies is invalid.

prefix specifies the characters that tempnam places at the start of the filename.

tempnam uses malloc to allocate space for the filename. You must free this space when it is no longer needed.

If successful, tempnam returns a pointer to the created filename. If an error occurs, tempnam returns the value NULL.

Example:

```
#include <stdio.h>

main()
{
    char *unique;

    if ((unique = tempnam("C:\\", "XYZ")) == NULL)
        printf("Error creating filename\n");
    else
        {
        printf("Filename created: %s\n", unique);
        free(unique);
        }
}
```

Related Functions: tmpfile, tmpnam

time

time_t **time**(time_t *current_time*);

Include file: <time.h>

Description:

time returns the number of seconds since midnight, 01/01/1970, Greenwich mean time.

current_time is a pointer to a variable to which time assigns the current time.

Example:

```
#include <time.h>

main()
{
    time_t current_time;

    time(&current_time);
    printf("Current system time is %s\n",
            ctime(&current_time));
}
```

Related Functions: asctime, ftime, gmtime, localtime, tzset, utime

tmpfile

FILE ***tmpfile**(void);

Include file: <stdio.h>

Description:

tmpfile creates a temporary file and returns a file pointer to that file.

tmpfile opens the file in binary read/write access mode ("w+b"). The file is automatically deleted when the file is closed, when the program terminates normally, or when rmtmp is called.

If successful, tmpfile returns a pointer to the file. If an error occurs, tmpfile returns the value NULL.

Example:

```
#include <stdio.h>

main()
{
    FILE *fp;
    int letter;

    if ((fp = tmpfile()) == NULL)
        printf("Error opening temporary file\n");
    else
        {
        for (letter = 'A'; letter <= 'Z'; letter++)
            putc(letter, fp);
        rewind(fp);
        while (! feof(fp))
            {
            letter = getc(fp);
            putchar(letter);
            }
        rmtmp();
        }
}
```

Related Functions: rmtmp, tempnam, tmpnam

tmpnam

char ***tmpnam**(char *unique_name);

Include file: <stdio.h>

Description:

tmpnam generates a temporary filename in the subdirectory defined by the P_tmpdir entry in the include file stdio.h.

unique_name is a pointer to the unique filename that tmpnam creates. If you pass a null pointer to tmpnam, it stores the filename in an internal buffer that is overwritten by subsequent calls.

If successful, tmpnam returns a pointer to the unique filename. If an error occurs, tmpnam returns the value NULL.

Example:

```
#include <stdio.h>
#include <stdlib.h>

main()
{
    char name[128];

    if (tmpnam(name) == NULL)
        printf("Error creating filename\n");
    else
        printf("Filename created: %s\n", name);
}
```

This program produces the following result:

```
Filename created: \2
```

Related Functions: tempnam, tmpfile

toascii

int **toascii**(int *letter*);

Include file: <ctype.h>

Description:

toascii sets all but the low-order 7 bits of an integer value to 0 so that the converted value represents an ASCII character set.

letter is an integer value to be converted into an ASCII character.

Example:

```
if (letter > 127)
    letter = toascii(letter);
```

Related Functions: tolower, toupper

tolower, _tolower

int **tolower**(int *letter*);

or

int **_tolower**(int *letter*);

Include file: <ctype.h>

Description:

tolower and _tolower convert an uppercase letter to lowercase.

letter is an uppercase letter to be converted to lowercase.

tolower converts a character to lowercase if the character represents an uppercase letter. If the letter is lowercase, tolower leaves it unchanged. The _tolower macro should be used only when a character is known to be uppercase; otherwise, the result is undefined.

Example: See toupper.

Related Functions: toascii, toupper

toupper, _toupper

int **toupper**(int *letter*);

or

int **_toupper**(int *letter*);

Include file: <ctype.h>

Description:

toupper and _toupper convert a lowercase letter to uppercase.

letter is a lowercase letter to be converted to uppercase.

toupper converts a character to uppercase if the character represents a lowercase letter. If the letter is uppercase, toupper leaves it unchanged. The _toupper macro should be used only when a character is known to be lowercase; otherwise, the result is undefined.

Example:

```
#include <ctype.h>
```

(continued)

```
main()
{
    char *str = "abcDEF#?*";

    while (*str)
        {
        printf("Letter %c toupper %c _toupper %c\n",
            *str, toupper(*str), _toupper(*str));
        str++;
        }
}
```

Related Functions: toascii, tolower

tzset

void **tzset**(void);

Include file: <time.h>

Description:

tzset assigns values to the global variables *daylight*, *timezone*, and *tzname* using the current environment setting for TZ.

TZ contains a three-letter time-zone name, an optional signed number that represents the difference in hours between Greenwich mean time and local time, and an optional daylight-saving-time zone. For example, PST8PDT is a valid TZ value for the Pacific time zone.

The global variable *daylight* is set to the value 1 if daylight-saving-time zone is specified in TZ; otherwise, *daylight* is set to 0.

The global variable *timezone* contains the difference in seconds between the current local time and Greenwich mean time.

The global variable *tzname* is a two-element array that points to the time-zone name and daylight-saving-time-zone name.

Example:

```
#include <time.h>

main()
{
    tzset();

    printf("Time-zone offset in seconds: %ld\n",
        timezone);
    printf("Time zone: %s   Daylight zone: %s\n",
        tzname[0], tzname[1]);
```

(continued)

```
if (daylight)
    printf("Daylight saving time is in effect\n");
else
    printf("Daylight saving time is not in effect\n");
}
```

Related Functions: asctime, ftime, gmtime, localtime, time

ultoa

char *__ultoa__(unsigned long int *value*, char *__ascii__, int *radix*);

Include file: <stdlib.h>

Description:

ultoa converts an unsigned long-integer value to its ASCII representation.

value is an unsigned long-integer value to be converted.

ascii is a character string to which the corresponding characters are assigned.

radix specifies the base of the output string. The value 2 is binary, 8 is octal, 10 is decimal, 16 is hexadecimal, and so on.

Example:

```
#include <stdlib.h>

main()
{
    unsigned long int value = 1;
    char buffer[128];
    int i;

    for (i = 1; i < 32; i++)
        printf("%ld in decimal is %s in binary\n",
                value << i, ultoa(value << i, buffer, 2));
}
```

Related Functions: itoa, ltoa

umask

int **umask**(int *permission*);

Include files: <io.h>, <sys\stat.h>, and <sys\types.h>

Description:

umask sets the program's file-permission mask.

The file-permission mask is used to modify the permission setting of new files created by the creat, open, or sopen function. If a bit in the permission mask is set to 1, the corresponding bit in the file's requested permission value is set to 0 (disallowed).

permission is one of the following values:

Value	*Meaning*
S_IREAD	no read access
S_IWRITE	no write access
S_IREAD ¦ S_IWRITE	no read or write access

Upon completion, umask returns the previous mask setting.

Example:

```
#include <sys\types.h>
#include <sys\stat.h>
#include <io.h>

main()
{
    printf("Default mask is %x\n", umask(S_IREAD));
}
```

Related Functions: chmod, creat, open

ungetc

int **ungetc**(int *letter*, FILE **file_pointer*);

Include file: <stdio.h>

Description:

ungetc returns a character to a specified input stream for later input processing.

letter is a character to be placed back into the input stream. ungetc does not allow you to ''unget'' an end-of-file character.

file_pointer is a file pointer associated with a file through the fdopen, fopen, or freopen function. ungetc returns the character to the input stream associated with the file pointer.

If successful, ungetc returns the character it returned to the input stream. If an error occurs, ungetc returns the value EOF.

Example:

```
letter = fgetc(fp);
if (isalpha(letter))
    putchar(letter);
else
    ungetc(letter, fp);
```

Related Functions: getc, putc

ungetch

int **ungetch**(int *letter*);

Include file: <conio.h>

Description:

ungetch returns a character to the input stream from stdin for later input processing.

letter is a character to be placed back into stdin's input stream. The character cannot be an end-of-file character.

If successful, ungetch returns the character it returned to the input stream. If an error occurs, ungetch returns the value EOF.

Example:

```
#include <conio.h>
#include <ctype.h>

main()
{
    int letter;

    letter = getchar();
    if (isalnum(letter))
        /* statements */
    else
        ungetch(letter);
    /* statements */
}
```

Related Functions: getc, getchar, ungetc

unlink

int **unlink**(const char ∗*pathname*);

Include file: <io.h> or <stdio.h>

Description:

unlink deletes a specified file.

pathname is a character string that contains the complete pathname of the file to be deleted.

If successful, unlink returns the value 0. If an error occurs, unlink returns the value −1 and sets the global variable *errno* to one of the following values:

Value	Meaning
EACESS	access denied—file is read-only
ENOENT	file not found

Example:

```
#include <io.h>

main(int argc, char *argv[])
{
    if (unlink(argv[1]) == -1)
        printf("Error deleting %s\n", argv[1]);
    else
        printf("%s successfully deleted\n", argv[1]);
}
```

Related Function: remove

utime

int **utime**(char ∗*pathname*, struct utimbuf ∗*stamp*);

Include files: <sys\types.h> and <sys\utime.h>

Description:

utime sets a file's date-and-time stamp.

pathname is a character string that contains the complete subdirectory path to the desired file.

stamp is a pointer to a structure that contains a file's date-and-time stamp. The include file utime.h defines the structure utimbuf as follows:

```
struct utimbuf
    {
    time_t actime;
    time_t modtime;
    };
```

If the stamp points to NULL, utime sets the file's date-and-time stamp to the current time.

If successful, utime returns the value 0. If an error occurs, utime returns the value −1 and sets the global variable *errno* to one of the following values:

Value	*Meaning*
EACESS	access denied—file is read-only
EINVAL	time-stamp argument invalid
EMFILE	too many open files
ENOENT	file not found

Example:

```
#include <sys\types.h>
#include <sys\utime.h>
#include <stdio.h>

main(int argc, char *argv[])
{
    if (utime(argv[1], NULL) == -1)
        printf("Error modifying %s\n", argv[1]);
    else
        printf("File stamp set to current date/time\n");
}
```

Related Functions: asctime, ctime, fstat, ftime, gmtime, localtime, stat, time

va_arg

va_arg(va_list *argument_ptr*, *type*);

Include file: <stdarg.h> or <varargs.h>

Description:

va_arg returns the next argument in a variable-length list of parameters.

va_arg works in conjunction with va_start to access parameters passed to functions in a variable-length list of parameters.

va_arg is a macro that returns the value of the next argument of the specified type and increments the argument pointer to point to the next argument.

Example: See va_start.

Related Functions: va_end, va_start

va_end

void **va_end**(va_list *argument_ptr*);

Include file: <stdarg.h> or <varargs.h>

Description:

va_end sets the argument pointer used by va_arg to NULL after the function accesses the last argument in a variable-length list of arguments.

argument_ptr is an argument pointer used by va_arg to access successive arguments.

Related Functions: va_arg, va_start

va_start

void **va_start**(va_list *argument_ptr*, *previous_parameter*);   ANSI

or

void **va_start**(va_list *argument_ptr*);   UNIX System V

Include file: <stdarg.h> or <varargs.h>

Description:

va_start marks the first parameter in a variable-length list of arguments to a function.

argument_ptr is an argument pointer used by va_arg to determine the current position within the variable-length list of parameters.

previous_parameter is the variable that precedes the start of the variable-length list of parameters. Inclusion of *previous_parameter* is required for ANSI compatibility.

Example:

```
#include <stdarg.h>
#include <stdio.h>

main()
{
    void display(int, ...);

    display(1, 10);
    display(2, 10, 20);
    display(3, 10, 20, 30);
}

void display(int count, ...)
{
    int i;
    va_list argument_ptr;

    va_start(argument_ptr, count);
    for (i = 1; i <= count; i++)
        printf("%d\n", va_arg(argument_ptr, int));
}
```

Related Functions: va_arg, va_end

vfprintf

int **vfprintf**(FILE *file_pointer*, const char *format_specification*,
           va_list *argument_ptr*);

Include file: <stdarg.h> or <varargs.h>

Description:

vfprintf formats and outputs data to a file by using a pointer to a variable-length list of arguments.

vfprintf uses the format specification to determine the number of arguments to be output to a file.

file_pointer is a file pointer associated with the output file through the fdopen, fopen, or freopen function.

format_specification is a character string that defines the output format used by vfprintf. Also see printf.

argument_ptr is a pointer to the first argument in the list of parameters to be output. This value is returned by either va_start or va_arg.

Example:

```
#include <stdio.h>
#include <stdarg.h>
#include <stdlib.h>

main()
{
    /* statements */
    error_handler("Error accessing file\n");
    error_handler("Error accessing %s\n", "TEST.DAT");
    error_handler("Error accessing %s; status %d\n",
                  "TEST.DAT", errno);
}

error_handler(char *format, ...)
{
    va_list argument_ptr;

    va_start(argument_ptr, format);
    vfprintf(stderr, format, argument_ptr);
}
```

Related Functions: vprintf, vsprintf

vprintf

int **vprintf**(const char *format_specification*, va_list *argument_ptr*);

Include file: <stdarg.h> or <varargs.h>

Description:

vprintf formats and outputs data to stdout by using a pointer to a variable-length list of arguments.

vprintf is identical to vfprintf except that vprintf writes to stdout and vfprintf writes to a file.

Example: See vfprintf.

Related Functions: vfprintf, vsprintf

vsprintf

int **vsprintf**(char *buffer*, const char *format_specification*,
      va_list *argument_ptr*);

Include file: <stdarg.h> or <varargs.h>

Description:

vsprintf formats and outputs data to a character string by using a pointer to a variable-length list of arguments.

vsprintf is identical to vfprintf except that vsprintf outputs to a character string and vfprintf writes to a file.

Example: See vfprintf.

Related Functions: vfprintf, vprintf

_wrapon

short far **_wrapon**(short *wrapflag*);

Include file: <graph.h>

Description:

_wrapon controls whether text written to an output window by _outtext is wrapped or truncated when it reaches the right margin of the window.

wrapflag specifies whether text is wrapped or truncated within the window. Values and corresponding meanings are as follows:

Value	*Meaning*
_GWRAPON	text wrapped within the window
_GWRAPOFF	text truncated

Upon completion, _wrapon returns the previous wrap setting.

Example:

```
#include <graph.h>
```

(continued)

```
main()
{
    char buffer[128];
    int i, j;

    _settextwindow(10, 10, 15, 60);
    for (i = 0; i < 10; i++)
        for (j = 0; j < 50; j++)
            {
            itoa(j, buffer, 10);
            _outtext(buffer);
            }
    _settextwindow(18, 10, 24, 60);
    _wrapon(_GWRAPOFF);
    for (i = 0; i < 10; i++)
        for (j = 0; j < 50; j++)
            {
            itoa(j, buffer, 10);
            _outtext(buffer);
            }
}
```

Related Functions: _outtext, _settextwindow

write

int **write**(int *file_handle*, char **buffer*, unsigned int *num_bytes*);

Include file: <io.h>

Description:

write writes the specified number of bytes from a buffer to a specified file.

file_handle is a file handle associated with an output file through the creat or open function.

buffer is a buffer that contains the data to be output.

num_bytes specifies the number of bytes to be output.

If successful, write returns the number of bytes actually written to the file. If an error occurs, write returns the value −1 and sets the global variable *errno* to one of the following:

Value	Meaning
EBADF	invalid file handle
ENOSPC	disk full

Example: See read.

Related Functions: close, creat, open, read

---

y0, y1, yn

See bessel.

Kris Jamsa

Kris Jamsa graduated from the United States Air Force Academy with a degree in computer science in 1983. Upon graduation, he moved to Las Vegas, Nevada, where he began work as a VAX/VMS system manager for the U.S. Air Force. In 1986, Jamsa received a master's degree in computer science, with an emphasis on operating systems, from the University of Nevada, Las Vegas. He then taught computer science at the National University in San Diego, California, for one year before leaving the Air Force in 1988 to begin writing full-time. He is the author of more than a dozen books on DOS, OS/2, Windows, hard-disk management, and Pascal and C programming languages. Jamsa currently resides in Las Vegas with his wife and two daughters.

OTHER TITLES FROM MICROSOFT PRESS

MICROSOFT® QUICKC® PROGRAMMING
The Microsoft Guide to Using the QuickC Compiler

The Waite Group: Mitchell Waite, Stephen Prata,
Bryan Costales, and Harry Henderson

MICROSOFT QUICKC PROGRAMMING is an authoritative introduction to every significant element of Microsoft QuickC. A detailed overview of the language elements gets you started. And the scores of programming examples and tips show you how to manipulate QuickC's variable types, decision structures, functions, and pointers; how to program using the Graphics Library; how to port Pascal to QuickC; how to interface your QuickC programs with assembly language; how to use the powerful source-level debugger; and more. If you're new to C or familiar with Microsoft QuickBASIC or Pascal, MICROSOFT QUICKC PROGRAMMING is for you. If you're a seasoned programmer, you'll find solid, reliable information that's available nowhere else.

650 pages, softcover, $21.95   Order Code 86-97633

PROFICIENT C
The Microsoft Guide to Intermediate and Advanced C Programming

Augie Hansen

"A beautifully conceived text, clearly written and logically organized...
a superb guide."   **Computer Book Review**

If you want to combine C with MS-DOS to produce powerful programs that run at astonishing speeds, PROFICIENT C is where you want to start. It contains a wealth of programming insights, professional know-how, and techniques to improve your programming skills. PROFICIENT C is a rich assortment of reliable, structured programming methods for designing, coding, and testing your programs. You'll discover clear, immediately useful information on the MS-DOS development environment, standard libraries and interfaces, and file- and screen-oriented programs. Here are dozens of modules and full-length utilities that you'll use again and again. Each one is practical and creative without being gimmicky. Included are programs that use sound and text-oriented visual effects and that control printer modes and screen color. Other programs update file modification times, test the driver, view and print files, and display non-ASCII text.

512 pages, softcover, $22.95   Order Code 86-95710

MICROSOFT® MOUSE PROGRAMMER'S REFERENCE
Microsoft Press

Currently attached to more than one million personal computers, the
Microsoft Mouse is one of the world's most popular PC peripherals
and an industry standard. No software program—custom or commer-
cial—is complete without support for the Microsoft Mouse. This
guide—by a team of experts from the Hardware Division of Microsoft
Corporation—enables intermediate- to advanced-level programmers
to add mouse support to their programs, thus adding value and ease of
use. It's both an essential reference to the mouse programming interface and a handbook for writing functional mouse menus. The two
5.25-inch companion disks include:

- MOUSE.LIB and EGA.LIB
- Microsoft Mouse menus
- a collection of valuable programs in BASIC, QuickBASIC, QuickC,
  Microsoft C, Pascal, Microsoft Macro Assembler, and FORTRAN

The MICROSOFT MOUSE PROGRAMMER'S REFERENCE is the
most authoritative and value-packed reference guide on mouse programming available.

336 pages, softcover with two 5.25-inch disks, $29.95
Order Code 86-97005

ADVANCED MS-DOS® PROGRAMMING, 2nd Edition
The Microsoft Guide for Assembly Language and C Programers
Ray Duncan

"ADVANCED MS-DOS PROGRAMMING *is one of the most
authoritative in its field…*"   **PC Magazine**

ADVANCED MS-DOS PROGRAMMING has been completely
revised and expanded to include MS-DOS version 4, DOS and OS/2
compatibility issues, and the new PS/2 ROM BIOS services. Ray Duncan begins his instructive guide to assembly language and C programming in the PC/MS-DOS environment with an overview of the
structure and loading of MS-DOS. He addresses key programming
topics, including character devices, mass storage, memory management, and process management. You will find a detailed reference
section of system functions and interrupts for all current versions of
MS-DOS; information on the ROM BIOS and on programming for the
EGA, VGA, PC/AT, and PS/2; information on programming with version 4.0 of the Lotus/Intel/Microsoft Expanded Memory Specification; and advice on writing "well-behaved" *vs* hardware-dependent

applications. The examples, ranging from programming samples to full-length utilities, are both instructive and utilitarian and were developed using the Microsoft Macro Assembler version 5.1 and the Microsoft C Compiler version 5.1.

688 pages, softcover, $24.95   Order Code 86-96668

THE MS-DOS® ENCYCLOPEDIA

Foreword by Bill Gates, Microsoft Corporation

"…for those with any technical involvement in the PC industry, this is the one and only volume worth reading."   **PC Week**

If you're a serious MS-DOS programmer, this is the ultimate reference. THE MS-DOS ENCYCLOPEDIA is an unmatched sourcebook for version-specific technical data, including annotations of more than 100 system function calls, each accompanied by C-callable, assembly language routines; for comprehensive version-specific descriptions and usage information on each of the 90 user commands— the most comprehensive guide ever assembled; and for documentation of a host of key programming utilities. Articles cover debugging methods, TSRs, installable device drivers, application writing for upward compatibility, and much, much more. THE MS-DOS ENCYCLOPEDIA contains hundreds of hands-on examples and thousands of lines of code, plus an index to commands and topics. Covering MS-DOS through version 3.2, with a special section on version 3.3, this encyclopedia is the preeminent, most authoritative reference for every professional MS-DOS programmer.

1600 pages, 7³/₈ x 10, hardcover, $134.95   Order Code 86-96122
softcover, $69.95   Order Code 86-96940

The manuscript for this book was prepared and submitted to
Microsoft Press in electronic form. Text files were processed
and formatted using Microsoft Word.

Cover design by Thomas A. Draper
Interior text design by Greg Hickman
Principal typography by Lisa Iversen

Text composition by Microsoft Press in Times Roman with
display in Times Roman Bold, using the Magna composition
system and the Linotronic 300 Laser imagesetter.